Rainbow Over My House

an incredible story of triumphant
victory over autism!

Rainbow Over My House

an incredible story of triumphant
victory over autism!

Author: Sheila Clayton Christie

Foreword By Dr. Julie Buckley, Md

Foreword By Bishop George L. Davis

WestBow
P R E S S
A DIVISION OF THOMAS NELSON

ISBN: 978-1-4497-5333-7 (e)
ISBN: 978-1-4497-5332-0 (sc)
ISBN: 978-1-4497-5331-3 (hc)

Library of Congress Control Number: 2012909167

WestBow Press books may be ordered through booksellers or by contacting:

WestBow Press
A Division of Thomas Nelson
1663 Liberty Drive
Bloomington, IN 47403
www.westbowpress.com
1-(866) 928-1240

Unless otherwise indicated, all scripture quotations are taken from The King James Version of the Holy Bible.

Printed in the United States of America

WestBow Press rev. date:6/6/2012

Contents

Dedication

This book is dedicated to my son, Daniel whose life has greatly impacted mine. You inspired me to step out of every comfort zone, embrace courage, face and overcome fears, withstand the so-called giants of life, and refuse to be denied! I live life today with a greater sense of purpose, destiny, and most of all faith, having mounted up on eagles' wings! I'm in awe of the miracle that you are, as you laugh, talk, and commune with me each day. I love you!

My family who made a great sacrifice and allowed me the time that I needed while working on the book.

Special Thanks To:

My mother Delores Ward Clayton, and my father, the late Arthur Clayton Sr. who went home to be with the Lord in February 2011, for being such supportive parents and wonderful grandparents. I certainly cannot forget my siblings: Arthur Jr., Renee' Clayton Price, Vincent Clayton, and Otis Holcomb.

Dr. Julie Buckley and the Pediatric Partners of Ponte Vedra staff.

Bishop George and Pastor April Davis, and the ministerial staff of Faith Christian Center, Jacksonville, Florida.

All of the therapists, specialists, and teachers who have been a part of Daniel's successful recovery.

Ms. Lucille, the singers and musicians who traveled with my family and I as we ministered in music.

All of the pastors, friends, and relatives who prayed and believed with us for a miracle!

And a special thanks to my son, Richard III, who persisted on January 23, 2009, and made sure that I saw the rainbow that was over our house.

Foreword

Dr. Julie Buckley, MD

Miracles

Every time I meet a new child with autism in my office, I pray. I pray that the family will remain intact, and that the siblings will get what they need as they grow up in a special needs home. I pray that the child will regain their health. I pray that they will find the joy in living on earth as a child. I pray that they will be able to communicate. I pray for their healing.

When Sheila Christie walked into my office, I was struck by her amazing spirit. She was both troubled and yet incredibly peaceful in her quest for answers to what happened to her son and what she was going to need to do to get him back.

What is so very special about Daniel, and his family, and their pursuit of recovery, is that it feels very much to me to have been less about what we've done in the office and the methods we've employed to foster healing, and instead, it's been much more about prayer and God.

When I think of Daniel, who has had remarkable recovery, the word Miracle comes to mind. His momma has prayed him well, and God has answered her prayers. I suspect I am little more than a vehicle in this great communication between Sheila, Daniel, and God, but what an honor to be able to witness it!

Dr. Julie Buckley, MD
Pediatric Partners of Ponte Vedra

Foreword

Bishop George L. Davis

The first thing that comes to mind when thinking about the Christie family is "love never fails." Love is a force whose power is underestimated and underutilized. The kind of love that God has for people is sometimes all that is needed to pull our children, families, and other loved ones through life's obstacles.

Sheila Christie is an example of how a mother's love will generate unimagined strength, wisdom, courage, and determination when it comes to fighting for her children, whether it be against an enemy in the form of a person or otherwise.

I have had the honor of pastoring Sheila Christie and her family for many years, during which time we have been a part of this miracle through prayer, counseling support, and spiritual direction.

The Christie family's story is one of triumph and victory obtained through faith, prayer, and perseverance. The good news to the reader is that you too can experience miracles in your life, whether in a situation similar to the Christies, or any other type of situation.

I congratulate, commend, and rejoice with the Christie family for their victory. And I join them in giving praise and glory to the Most High God without whom none of it would have been possible.

Bishop George L. Davis
Senior Pastor
Faith Christian Center

Introduction

Daniel was a boy who had fun. When it came to playing, he could go for hours, non-stop. At the sight of his presence the room brightened, and filled with the sound of laughter. His hugs were bigger than life, and his kisses melted the heart of everyone he shared his love with.

Then, one day it all changed. Daniel lay still on the floor in a trance. Alive, yet unresponsive, his face no longer sparkled. There were no signs of giggling and laughter. Within a few days afterwards he lost his speech, hearing, and all cognitive functions. For twenty-four months, despite repeated doctor's visits and a hospitalization, the symptoms persisted and went undiagnosed.

As the family tried to cope and return to a normal lifestyle, the symptoms eventually culminated while on a family vacation at one of the nation's largest theme parks.

Convinced that the symptoms were related to a serious medical condition, Daniel's mother, Sheila, prayed for direction. Within a few days her answer came through a cover story of her local newspaper. With a new pediatrician, and finally a diagnosis, the journey through Autism began. For the next seven years of his life, he and his family experienced one of the most tumultuous challenges that they have ever faced.

As you read the detailed accounts of this story, feel the heart and soul of his mother as she relives the joy and pain of this journey, to provide hope to other families who are still waiting for a miracle. Experience her pain! Applaud her tenacity! Laugh out loud! Hear her resounding voice proclaiming that "Miracles still happen!" "Autism is treatable!" "Yes! It can be overcome!"

Dream Vacation

Can anything be more exciting to children than a family vacation? The idea of Mom packing the suitcases and allowing them to pack their favorite stuffed animal or toy can provoke an outburst of thrill and joy! Children are not usually concerned about the vacation destination. It's satisfying enough to know that they are going for a drive in the car, or going to the airport to ride an airplane. Do you remember moments like this from your childhood? What was one of your most memorable family vacations? What made it so special? What was the atmosphere like in the house during this time? It was probably charged with the energy that comes only from a child! We certainly experienced that same energy in our house!

"Nightlights, camera, double-stroller, blue blanket, dolls, and Barney! Are these items in the living room, yet?" "Yes, Mom everything's here!" said Richard. "Please don't forget the double-stroller!" I shouted out to him. "It's already in here!" He shouted back. "Okay, thanks." "You're welcome," he responded playfully.

What a wonderful little helper! I could have asked for anything, and he would have made sure that it was there, even if it meant he had to create it. Richie, as we affectionately called him was eight years old, my daughter Courtney was six, and Daniel four. They were more excited than a teacher going on summer break! It was vacation time in our house and the actual day when we would leave.

As most mothers do, I was finishing the packing of the suitcases in my room, while the children followed me, asking what seemed like 10,000 questions per minute. They were fidgety. They were bouncing and jumping instead of walking. There were lots of smiles and giggles. They were wired! My children had watched every Disney video in our collection at least twice within the prior two months in expectation of going on vacation. Without knowing our plans, they suggested every theme park they'd seen in the videos. My husband and I would laugh uncontrollably at their tactics to convince us to fulfill their requests. They had a list of demands, but didn't they know that we enjoyed surprising them? Well, we kept the destination a surprise until we were well on our way. It was March 2004, and they were about to experience the ultimate children's vacation at the Magic Kingdom!

It was a day that my husband and I looked forward to, when our children were old enough to walk through the Magic Kingdom and enjoy thrilling rides and attractions, dance to the music from their favorite Disney movies, eat delicious foods, and end it all with the big parade! Although we had been there about four times between the two of us, this time was going to be the "icing on the cake" because we would see it through the eyes of our children. We could only imagine the thrill when they'd see their favorite Disney characters come to life!

The trip was well planned for Spring Break. The hotel we reserved was within the vicinity of the main gate. We hardly slept the night before. Expectation and anticipation kept us whispering and laughing after we'd said, "Good Night" and turned off the lights. We took turns telling each other, "Shhh," only to provoke more laughter. Eventually we fell off to sleep.

The morning came quickly. The excitement from the night before carried over into the new day. The children got dressed in record time. No one lagged behind. After eating a continental breakfast we headed to our destination for a full day of unlimited fun.

We arrived at The Magic Kingdom around ten o'clock in the morning. After parking in "Donald," we rode the monorail into the park. With our park guides in hand, we walked in the direction of the rides that we knew our children would like to ride first. This would be our starting point, and eventually we would cover the entire park. We figured that we would be there for about ten hours or so, topping off the night with the magical parade. But boy, oh boy were we wrong! Unbeknownst to us, we were about to have an unforeseen encounter of the worst kind. Within a matter of minutes of walking into the park, things went terribly wrong! Daniel began to cry. He also put his hands over his ears as if he was either frightened, or because the music was too loud. Although I'd never seen or heard a child cry at Disney, we realized that this was his first visit there, and that it might take a few minutes to adjust to all of the excitement. So my husband picked him up and began asking him questions. "What's wrong Daniel?" "Why are you crying?" "Are you afraid?" "Is the music too loud?" "Do your ears hurt?" "Talk to me, tell daddy what's wrong." But Daniel didn't say anything, he just cried.

We decided to sit in the area near the carousel, which is one of his favorite rides. We relaxed as we observed him watching it go around and around. He seemed calm so we decided to ride the carousel, and then move on to more fun. But after the carousel ride ended he began crying again. We decided not to ride it again, because there was so much more to see and do, and we wanted them to have an unforgettable experience, one they would write about in school - "My Summer Vacation at Disney World." So we continued our day of walking through the Magic Kingdom, yet all the while Daniel continued to cry. Determined not to allow it to deter us from having fun, we went from ride to ride listening to him whimper.

Just when we thought that he had adjusted and was going to be fine, he took us by surprise by screaming out, and throwing a temper tantrum. He cried loudly and uncontrollably. I reached in my purse and pulled out a lollipop. I put it in his mouth, and he quickly began to chew it. After he finished it, I pulled out another one and gave it to him. As long as he was eating the candy he didn't cry, but when it was all gone, he started to cry again. Of course, we knew that giving him candy was not a good idea, but at that time we didn't have many options. We just wanted the crying to stop!

We noticed that we were now getting long stares from those around us. The expression on some of their faces read, "You are ruining our vacation. Either make him be quiet or leave!" We tried to be considerate of others, including our two other children who were also there to have fun. But we were so distracted trying to figure out what was wrong with Daniel, that Courtney and Richard were not enjoying themselves. They wanted to go on ride after ride, but once we were in line, Daniel would cry even louder. My husband and I took turns holding him until he would no longer come to me. Nearly five hours had passed and we were still trying to have fun.

Finally, we got up the nerve to get back in line to ride an attraction that we were really anticipating getting on. So we stood in line waiting for our turn. Then, Daniel really "let us have it!" The crying and screaming tantrum went to a whole new level! He began to kick, and sling his arms. He was leaning backwards and forwards trying to get down out of my husband's arms. He reached for me. He reached for Richard and Courtney. He even reached for the people in line. He was acting like a two year old who'd been told, "No!" and refused to accept it. Now, you can imagine how much attention this brought us. I was tired of this wrestling match! My nerves were on edge! My other children were unhappy and embarrassed! My husband was speechless! I would almost guarantee that we were soon to be confronted by their security staff. It was just that bad. So we chose to leave the park and go back to the hotel.

Once back at the hotel, my husband took Richard and Courtney to the swimming pool while Daniel and I laid down for a nap. As I lay there, I cried silently while asking myself questions: "What is going on with him?" "Why did he behave this way?" "He was totally out of character! There was nothing scary or startling that we exposed him to at the theme park. He was very comfortable with each of the Disney characters that we took pictures with, and we chose the rides carefully to make sure that they were age appropriate. He especially enjoyed "It's A Small World." I think it was the favorite ride of us all. "So what happened?" "What did he see or hear to make him act so terrible?" Even in mentally retracing the day, I couldn't figure it out. Things did not turn out as we planned. However, we were still able to make a few good memories of our time at the Magic Kingdom.

We stayed in Orlando for a few more days. Our outings were changed to places such as the movies, Chuck E Cheese's and the shopping malls. Each day ended with a swim in the pool. Although Daniel was peaceful, there were still obvious signs that we had a major issue on our hands, but of what? He was my "happy-happy" baby, my little bear hugger with drooling kisses, and a bundle of joy in every sense of the word. Pure delight! I enjoyed him so much that I would have considered having one more child, believing that he or she would be just like him.

At the end of the week we headed for home. Daniel peacefully slept most of the way. However, my mind was in a whirlwind of thoughts as I tried to determine the cause of his behavior. I reclined my seat and stared out of the window. As we continued on Interstate 4 towards home, I eventually fell off to sleep. It would be several days later before I would recall an incident that occurred two years earlier involving Daniel. That incident caused quite a scare to my entire household! Yet, we'd discover that its repercussions were manifesting two years later. What then followed was nothing short of a nightmare, leaving us in the dark groping for answers for two more years. This is where the journey began:

On June 18, 2002 all three of my children were playing on the floor in my bedroom while I stood in the adjacent bathroom combing my hair. They were laughing and having a great time, as they always did. I kept a close watch and stayed nearby because they were toddlers, and I didn't want anyone to get hurt. After I finished, I told them that, "I was done, and that their playtime was over." Everyone got up and ran out of my room except Daniel. He was lying on the floor on his back, staring at the ceiling. So I looked up at the ceiling to see what he was staring at, saw nothing, and again said to him, "Let's Go!" He still didn't respond, so I commenced to tickle him, which usually caused him to get up and run from me, hoping I'd catch him. However, there was still no response. I then knelt down next to him and looked into his eyes. He was in a trance! It was as if he slipped away into another world. I yelled to my husband for help. We called the pediatrician about the symptoms, and then rushed Daniel to the emergency room. He was immediately admitted and treated as priority . I stayed with him the entire time, answering the physician's questions regarding the incident, family medical history, and his individual medical history. Several times they questioned if we had a family history of seizures. Each time I responded, "No."

Over the next two days numerous tests were performed in hopes of diagnosing the symptoms. They all returned with negative results. According to the emergency room physician, "He was a fine healthy toddler who possibly had the wind knocked out of him while horse playing with his siblings, and to bring him back if his symptoms worsen, otherwise follow up with his pediatrician." I immediately reminded him that, "I was watching my children the entire time that they were playing, and there was no rough horse playing." He was surprised that I didn't just accept his diagnosis. I then explained to him that I was a stay at home mom, and the only caretaker he's ever had. Therefore if there was any incident or moment in his life that altered him in any way, I would be the first to know of it." I wasn't trying to be complicated, but on the other hand, this was my baby, and I needed an answer that made sense. It was hard enough to have needed to bring him to the emergency room, so I wasn't about to go back home without knowing that he was going to be well. "I told him simply that, "This is uncommon behavior for my little boy!" He didn't know what else to say, so I told him that, " I just want to make sure that everything possible had been done to help my son." He assured me that they performed every test necessary. We then went home.

Over the next several months Daniel regressed and experienced major health issues including loss of speech, cognitive and memory loss, loss of hearing, lack of eye contact, and refusal to potty train. He constantly cried and whined to communicate. He covered his ears with his hands as if all sound was too loud. He sat and played by himself in his own world as if we no longer existed. When he became excited, he quickly flapped his arms as if to imitate a bird, while turning around in circles.

Without a clue as to what was happening to Daniel, we were dumbfounded, yet determined to be there for him, and to get to the bottom of this madness! We could clearly see that he was very unhappy. Each day we tried to invoke communication from him by telling him to repeat certain phrases after us. Our efforts were ineffective. So, if he was hungry or thirsty, he no longer asked for what he wanted, but would hold my hand and lead me to the refrigerator or pantry. It would usually take several attempts before I picked the one that he was requesting.

Speaking of food, my once healthy little eater no longer had an appetite for fruits, vegetables, and the wholesome meals I cooked. He now craved starches. His diet consisted of only five foods: rice, corn, bread, mashed potatoes, and French fries. He disliked water, and would drink it only if I added a few drops of fruit juice.

Our weekly visits to the park became workout sessions as I repeatedly intercepted his wandering off by himself. When encouraged to play with his brother and sister or other children, he would begin to scream, and of course the children would run away from him. It was such a heartbreaker for me, because I desired him to make friends and to be liked by other children. But he couldn't help himself. Eventually even my children found it unbearable to deal with.

The intolerable behavior was beginning to have a ripple effect in every area of our lives. Our home atmosphere changed from being fun and relaxing, to tense and stressful. Trips to the mall or supermarket were cut short by his loud outbursts and screams.

Family outings and barbeques were usually interrupted by tantrums. I remember on two occasions, while performing live, Daniel pulled away from the babysitter and ran up on stage. I kept singing, while motioning to him to go back to his seat. At the other event he did the same thing, however, the host was not sensitive at all. His remarks about Daniel were very offensive and really hurt. I was angry at him, and never wanted to work with him again! But I eventually forgave him. I realized he had no idea what we were dealing with.

The next two years were full of frequent office visits. Sometimes we were at the pediatrician as often as four times a month. They thought I was overreacting. I thought they lacked answers for Daniel's symptoms but were too arrogant to admit it. And to make matters worse, because it was a pediatrician group, we almost never saw the same doctor. That is, not until I began to request the appointments on the day that the chief pediatrician was present.

On one particular visit, he told me that, "There is nothing to be concerned about at his age because this is typical behavior for boys; they are often slow developers." He continued to say that, "Daniel is the youngest child. You probably do everything for him. He's spoiled, and will talk again when he's ready. "

Now there was no way that I was going to accept his remarks as truth! I reminded him that, "My son was born a healthy, nine pound thirteen ounce baby, and that he was the discharging pediatrician that we chose to come to the hospital , which meant that he examined Daniel from head to toe, inside-out, and wrote him a 'clean bill of health.' The hospital allowed me to take my baby home on the day after he was born, because he was born healthy. I also reminded him of my six year old son, and four year old daughter who were also patients of his from their birth. They were born healthy, and never had any kind of developmental delays or challenges. They potty trained well, and transitioned out of their toddler years with ease." And yes, I know that no two children are alike, and that all children are vulnerable to common childhood diseases. But hello, hello, hello! Can you hear me? These were not the symptoms or signs of common childhood diseases such as chicken pox, measles, or asthma. Whatever this was, it was quite a monster! A hidden giant that certainly was not playing fair, because we didn't even know its name!

I ended the visit that day by telling the doctor that I was concerned about Daniel's hearing. I'd previously shared with a nurse friend of the family that Daniel seems to ignore me when I call his name, which was very unusual behavior for him. I shared how I recently had some girlfriends over for a fellowship, and I decided to "show him off." Whenever I called his name, he'd immediately stop whatever he was doing, and come running to me full speed, bear hug me, kiss me on the lips, and take off running! I knew that he was playing with toys, so I would purposefully wait until he was with his toys again, and I would call him for the second time. Without fail he'd come flying from his room, through the living room, into the family room and repeat our hugs and kisses ritual. I called him to me four times, and received the same response each time. We were all laughing because of his enthusiasm and consistency to respond each time I called him. We jokingly said, "We wish that all males responded in such a manner, that is, to come immediately, after being called." We enjoyed the humor, and because of that wonderful memory, and so many others similar to it, I had something to compare his current behavior to, which was anything but normal!

I didn't wait for the doctor to diagnose his hearing. Instead I requested a referral to an otolaryngologist. I refused to deal with anyone besides a specialist to check his ears. Enough was enough! No, I didn't know what was going on, but I knew that something different must be done. During our very first visit to the specialist, the tests performed determined that Daniel not only had a hearing impairment, but needed surgically implanted "tubes." His surgery was immediately scheduled. He would need to wear the "tubes" for two years.

The day of the surgery was quite an emotional one for me. My husband was there to support me, but still it was hard. I really did not want my little boy to experience any of the trauma that he was about to. What saddened me the most was that although we would be there with him when he was admitted, at some point it would be as far as we would be able to go. We would have to kiss him goodbye, and walk away listening to his screams for us to come back. Although we spoke with the specialist, and the anesthesiologist just minutes before the surgery, it was still a very tough moment for me. If there was an easier way that he could have had his hearing restored, I would have taken it. I just couldn't help remembering how afraid he looked when they were wheeling him out of the room.

About an hour later we were called back to the recovery area, where we spoke with both doctors again. They assured us that, "The surgery went well, and that Daniel's hearing should be restored completely as a result of wearing the tubes." Shortly afterwards, the anesthesiologist came to awaken him. Softly, repeatedly calling his name, he handled Daniel very gently. Daniel stirred at hearing his name. Immediately after waking up from the surgery, he saw my husband and I, and reached for us. He tried to get up, but the anesthesiologist refrained him. A few minutes later he gave him something to drink and performed a final examination before discharging him. As we were preparing to go home the surgeon gave us post-surgical care instructions, and warned us that, "Daniel probably would not be coherent, nor respond to us for at least four hours. He will be very sluggish, and will only want to sleep. This is the normal response for children following this surgical procedure." We then thanked him for a successful surgery, signed the discharge papers, and headed for home.

My husband and I had met at the surgical center, which meant that we were in separate vehicles. We decided that Daniel would ride home with him, and I would follow them. He often looked in the rearview mirror at Daniel, and thought it was interesting that instead of sleeping, he was wide awake. Then suddenly, without any prompting Daniel began to try to talk! He started by making loud one sentence sounds, and then added more as if he was having a conversation with Daddy. My husband called me on my cell phone and told me what was happening. He said that, "It nearly scared the living daylights out of him!" He asked me what to do! I told him to, "Talk back to him!" " Hold a conversation!" " Say, yes that's right Daniel!" I was driving with tears of joy flowing down my face. I wanted so much to be in the car with them! When we arrived home I ran to the car to see Daniel, and sure enough he looked at me and included me in the conversation. Later that afternoon the surgeon called to check on Daniel. When I told him what we experienced, and that Daniel was still wide awake, he responded that, "Although it was not the 'normal response,' it certainly was great to hear, and to call his office if there were any surgery related concerns."

Over the next few days, I began to look for ways to capitalize on his progress. I wanted something that would promote more language and actual words, so I prayed and asked God to help me. Give me direction because I didn't know where to start looking. Although I was a stay- at- home mom, I didn't have a lot of extra time to research. Especially since all three of my children were home with me.

The thought came to me to go to the nearest toy store to see what was available in their educational video section. I was speechless! I knew that thought did not come from me. It was also not coincidental that I live seven minutes from the most popular toy store in America. Well, God certainly answered my prayer, because I found exactly what I needed for Daniel. I bought two Brainy Baby videos: Talking videos with classical music in the background - a perfect combination. These videos also were for infants and toddlers, ages 3-18 months who were speaking their first words. While reading this information, I suddenly had an emotional moment, nearly talking myself out of buying them, because Daniel was four. I finally kicked my ego to the curb and took the videos home to my son. I decided to introduce only one video the first week, and would add the other once I saw that he was ready for more. So, we silently watched the first video together, and then I got up to cook dinner. I decided to play it again, since Daniel was still sitting in the family room as if he was waiting for me to press play. While cooking, all of a sudden I heard him repeat the person talking on the video. I quietly, yet quickly walked up behind him to observe him, and yes, he was repeating what was being said on the video. I scared him when I began to clap and jump for joy. Afterwards he continued to watch the video while I called my husband at work to share the good news.

I felt so empowered! It was a big step in the right direction! It was also the moment that I believed Daniel was not going to be like this always. He would be his normal self again. I also realized that I was his advocate now, in the driver's seat, which is where we parents need to be when it comes to the welfare of our children. No, we may not know as much as the physician or surgeon that's working with our child, and we are not required to, otherwise we could "fix" them. But we as parents know our children, and even when we are not sure of the cause, or cure for their pain, our gut feeling doesn't rest until we find the remedy and make it right!

So I was on a mission! Destination healing! But healing of what?

Giant Exposed vs. Giant Revealed

The morning of April 29, 2004 seemed no different than any other morning. I woke up and started my daily routine: devotion , shower and dress, make breakfast, and wake up the children. After breakfast we took the two older children to school. Daniel and I filled the day with different activities.

Later that evening, I went to the store alone to buy more pull-ups. I always took the longest route because it allowed more time to be by myself. This was also the time when I could really cry and pour out my heart. If I felt like screaming or beating the steering wheel, it was okay because I was alone. This was also the time when I would treat myself to junk food: chips, an oatmeal crème pie, and a banana icee. These foods actually calmed my emotions. They worked like a drug. I would never have told anyone what I was eating, because everyone who knew me, knew that I was not only a vegetarian, but most importantly serious about good health. Nevertheless, to continue my routine, I stopped at the convenience store for junk food. The checkout line was unusually long.

As I waited my turn, I became impatient and began to look around at different displays in the store. My eyes met the local newspaper stand. Now, I am not a newspaper subscriber, but I usually purchase one during the holidays to see the latest gift ideas. As the line grew closer to the register, I could see the pictures on the front page of the newspaper: One of a mother and daughter, and the other, a mother and her three sons. I could also see the headlines: "Children Denied Immunity." I didn't understand what it meant, so I picked it up and began to read. By the time I finally got to the cashier , I was speechless and my eyes were quickly swelling with tears. I made it to my van, put my head down and cried. The newspaper story was about two families whose children were suffering horrific symptoms after being vaccinated. The symptoms included: loss of speech, loss of hearing, low cognitive ability, developmental delays, and much more. It seemed that these children who were once thriving and developing well, slipped into a cognitive "fog" and begin regressing. The regression was huge, two or more years, causing some to return to diapers and infant-like tendencies, leaving parents and physicians stunned and without answers, again with the initial onset pointing back to the children's immunization. The families were sharing their story to raise public awareness, and hopefully save other families from experiencing this nightmare.

After reading the article again, I sat quietly and reminisced about the last two years of our lives. It had been very challenging, and all we wanted were answers. There were so many similarities between Daniel's symptoms, and the children's, in the newspaper article. I realized that my trip to the store was no coincidence on that evening, but it was for the sole purpose of bringing me to the moment where I would find the answer to what I'd been praying for. All of the sleepless nights, lying there crying silently on my pillow in the dark. Sometimes standing over my little one watching him sleep and hoping that he would wake up and just snap out of it. The months of anger and anguish. Long stares and whispers. And then it all changes in just one day!

When I returned home, I shared the news with my husband. We rejoiced to know that we not only had some answers, but also directions. The article listed the name of the only pediatrician in Northeast Florida who was treating children with these symptoms for the purpose of helping them to recover. Also listed was the name of the attorneys handling claims, and other information. I called the journalist who wrote the story and told him how grateful I was for the article, and that my son had several of the symptoms listed. He was very appreciative of the feedback, and suggested that I call the attorneys first. I called one of the attorneys, and he enlightened me more about what was shared in the newspaper article. He told me that, "The symptoms were being diagnosed as vaccine injuries. The harmful ingredient was the mercury-based preservative, Thimersal." I was also informed that, "We were the sixty-first family in Jacksonville to report these symptoms to him, and that there were many other families facing these challenges, but hadn't reported them yet because they were misdiagnosed. In the United States, over 3,700 families had recently reported these same symptoms to their pediatrician, and thousands more were expected." We ended the conversation by scheduling an appointment, and his referring me to the pediatrician in the article, Dr. Julie Buckley.

On May 19, 2004 Daniel and I walked into the office of Pediatric Partners of Ponte Vedra. We were immediately warmed by the mural of jungle animals on the wall. With Daniel being an animal lover, he began to flap his hands and twirl around in excitement. Dr. Buckley entered the waiting room with her eyes fixed on him. He jumped up and down, and walked on his "tippy toes" from one side of the room to the other looking at as many animals as possible. He uttered loud "sounds" as if he was trying to say something about them. He pointed at them and touched them. Dr. Buckley formally introduced herself, then resumed to observing Daniel. He did not acknowledge her presence, nor respond when she called his name. So she knelt down, held his hands, turned his head to make eye contact with her, and began to gently talk to him. He immediately turned his head, so she turned his head towards her again, and this time held his face with both hands. He looked at her for a brief second, but could not keep eye contact, even with her holding his face. He whined and pulled away, returning to the mural of animals.

She then invited me to sit in her office, while we kept Daniel in view as he played. She and I had previously spoken in my initial telephone call, so she was aware of some of Daniel's symptoms. However, I would still rehearse the entire story dating back to the hospitalization in 2002, which was just a few weeks after his MMR (Measles, Mumps, and Rubella) immunization. After hearing my story, she asked me questions regarding my pregnancy with Daniel: "How was your pregnancy?" I responded, "Easy. I enjoyed it. I did not experience "morning sickness" this time. I was energetic, led a normal lifestyle, and even stayed calm when hurricane Floyd threatened the area. However I was treated for early labor at about 30 weeks. I was given an injection to stop the contractions. "How was your delivery?" It was induced, and all went well. There were no complications. "Tell me about Daniel's progression from there." I shared with her how Daniel had such a remarkable beginning. He was advancing so quickly that I often said to him, "Hey little poogee what's your hurry? Mommy can't 'take it' if you grow up too fast." He would then look at me and smile as if he understood exactly what I said. He began talking at around nine months. He often humored us at bedtime, because he was selective with his prayer partner. He did not allow me nor my husband to pray with him two nights in a row. I often tried to ignore his specifics for the sake of just going to bed, but when I would kneel next to him he would say to me, "No Daddy." Meaning it was Daddy's turn. So I would go and get my husband and tell him that Daniel was waiting for him to come and listen to him say his prayers. I want to emphasize here that Daniel only wanted us to listen to him pray. He did not want us to verbalize. We were to remain silent. We'd taught him to say the model prayer, aka "The Lord's Prayer," and although he was less than a year old, he did not want our help! We were there to assist only if he got stuck. If we tried to pray with him, or hurry him as he took his time, he would stop praying, and sarcastically look at us. My husband and I would be totally amused by his audacity. Once we were alone we would say something like, "He has a lot of nerve. He hasn't been alive long enough to be so demanding." And then we'd laugh over and again.

This was one of the key indicators that something was wrong with Daniel. I remember kneeling next to him shortly after his MMR (Measles, Mumps and Rubella) vaccination, and he could not remember the words, and struggled to even repeat them after me. He eventually lost his speech, and memory of that prayer.

I went on to share with Dr. Buckley, that because he was always in someone's arms, Daniel was more than a year old when he mastered walking. He was such a gorgeous, handsome little guy, and was always being held by friends and family. Always sitting on someone's lap, whether at church, or family gatherings. However at home, you almost couldn't keep up with him. He loved to run through the house, despite our "No running in the house" rule. We'd laugh, as he would lean his head to the side as he ran around a corner. As a precaution, when I cooked, I put up gates at both entrances to the kitchen.

He played well with his siblings. And although he hadn't learned to share his toys, he was pretty good at trading. He loved books at an early age, and enjoyed watching his favorite children's educational television shows. Because I resigned from Corporate America one month before conceiving him, he had never been enrolled in a daycare facility. I resigned to be at home to care for my children, and was blessed to do so.

On the subject of food, he was a healthy eater. Mealtime was pretty easy. He also cooperated well at snack time, not begging for sugary treats. Besides, he would not have found any if he had. I narrowed their cookies to graham crackers and animal crackers. All other snacks were fruit, popcorn, peanut butter crackers, etc. Fast food was seen only in the television commercials. Never on his plate.

I summarized Daniel's history by talking about his sleep pattern. He was a good sleeper. He usually slept ten to twelve hours per night, with a starting bedtime of seven – thirty pm. He did not wake up in the middle of the night. He was also a sound sleeper. I mentioned his being a sound sleeper, because as a songwriter and recording artist, I usually recorded at night after I put my children in bed. They couldn't help but hear me singing, and the music playing, yet they never woke up. We'd check on them often to make sure that the volume was not too loud, and each time they were always sound asleep.

At the end of my conversation Dr. Buckley then evaluated Daniel. He did not cooperate at all. He squirmed from the moment she measured his height and weight to every procedure that followed. He was reluctant to sitting still, and began to whine and pull my fingers away from his so that he could get away from me, so at some point I just held him so that she could complete her touching part of the evaluation. Afterwards, she began a conversation with him, and he did everything possible to get away from us, never making eye contact with her. She then said that, "It was okay to let him go," and he took off running like a freed stallion, right back to the animal mural. Flapping, twirling, turning and "barking. "He was happy again to be left alone doing what he wanted to do, in his own world. I felt like I had just had a low impact workout session. For a brief second or so, we both sat there silently staring at him. The silence was broken by Dr. Buckley's words: "Sheila, Daniel has autism." "He has what?" I replied, "Autism." "What is autism?" I asked. "Autism is a bio-neurological developmental disability that generally appears before the age of three, and impacts the normal development of the brain in the areas of social interaction, communication skills and cognitive function. There are usually difficulties in verbal and non-verbal communication, social interactions, and leisure or play activities. The occurrence is one in every 150 children born in the U.S., and four out of five of those children are boys. It is also believed that the onset can be attributed to mercury poisoning, which links to childhood vaccinations. Daniel will have to be tested in order to determine if he has mercury poisoning, and we need to make it a priority! Timing is very key in the treatment of autism. Autism is treatable. It can be overcome!"

At that point, I felt like my spirit left my body. I could still see and hear Dr. Buckley talking, but I felt as if I'd slipped into a dark vacuum and was falling further into it. My thoughts were confused.

I was screaming out, but no one could hear me. I was staring at her, yet captured inside of her previous statement that my son's symptoms were related to a horrible condition that was not only unfamiliar, but also unexplainable. Eventually I was able to refocus in time to hear her say, "In the treatment of autism there is a window, and we need to keep that in mind." "What do you mean a window?" I asked. "There is a window of time during which if he is aggressively treated for these symptoms, we can pull him out of autism. There are numerous treatments, therapies and procedures that may be required to get him there, but recovery is possible, and that's our goal for Daniel. Total Recovery!"

Tears began to roll down my cheeks. I tried not to cry, but I needed to! I was so hurt! Angry and confused! Like a 500 pound weight had just been put on my chest. My heart felt like it was going to burst through. I didn't understand how something like this could happen to my little boy. I was even angrier at all of the pediatricians who were uninformed about autism, misdiagnosing my son's symptoms. Some of them saw him repeatedly over the two year period that we were asking for help! They never tried to further research to see if his symptoms were related to more than just their diagnosis of "The Typical American Boy."

Dr. Buckley could see how hurt I was. She then began to share with me her "story." Not only was she a pediatrician treating children with autism and vaccine injuries, but she was also the mother of a child with these symptoms. She unknowingly administered a vaccination to her daughter that contained the mercury-based preservative, Thimerosal, Her daughter was now being treated for autism. But Dr. Buckley's attitude and outlook regarding her daughter's future was positive, packed with teeth gritting tenacity and energy, not to be reckoned with! She told me that, "She was believing for college graduation, and wedding invitations!" And, "That I could borrow her statement and believe the same way for Daniel, because this diagnosis is not the end of their story! They will overcome every symptom! They will recover and lead successful, productive, happy lives!

Not only did I agree with her, but I soon found out that this was Julie's (as we affectionately call her) overall personality: tenacious, energetic, daring, a lover of children, and a giver of oneself on the behalf of others. She purposes to see families healed!

On that day, May 19, 2004, the giant was finally exposed! We now knew what we were up against, and most importantly we knew its name. Autism. For two years it had bullied our lives, and watched us struggle for answers, but now everything was about to change, because there was another giant stepping up to the plate! A new giant revealed! One coming out of obscurity! Like David who slew Goliath! He was the unforeseen, unlikely opponent that saw that there was a cause to stand up to his giant. And he did, because there was a giant on the inside of him! So I realized that despite how I felt, this was not a time for fear, but of courage. Daniel needed me to be strong! Cry, but get up and fight! So just like David, the giant in me was revealed that day! I made a pact with my son that I would fight for him! I was ready and willing to do whatever was needed to restore my son! I was determined that we too would see college graduation, wedding invitations, grandchildren, Victory!

Step by Step

We came home from our initial visit to Dr. Buckley with plenty of information and homework. Her first instructions were to, "Take all gluten and casein (dairy) foods out of Daniel's diet, and replace them with foods that were gluten free and casein free (GF/CF). It is possible that he had mercury poisoning from his vaccination, and if so, the mercury would have caused damage to the gut. The gut is the home base for the immune system, and if damaged by mercury, it's possible that it would be unable to process certain proteins.

I scheduled his first blood draw to determine if there was mercury in his little body. I was often reminded that these symptoms did not manifest until after his MMR vaccination, so I was eager to find out!

I also went on my first shopping trip to purchase GF/CF foods. I went to one of our natural foods supermarkets in the area. As soon as I entered the produce area, I was greeted by one of the employees. She said to me, "Let me know if I can assist you in any way." I immediately told her that, "It was my first time shopping there, and that I was looking for GF/CF foods for my little boy." She smiled and asked, "Is he one of Dr. Buckley's patients?" I told her, "Yes!" She then said that, "Many of Dr. Buckley's patients shop there, and as a result of it, they often meet other families from her office, compare stories, and form friendships." We then toured the entire store. It was very easy to find the foods that were GF/CF, because all of the shelves were marked with special labels. If the label was yellow and orange, it read, "gluten free and casein free." There were even shelves marked "peanut free." Their label was green. I thanked her for the tour, and then went shopping. I was able to replace all of Daniel's foods, including: rice, bread, meats, grits, pasta, butter, waffles, chips, applesauce, fruit juices, cookies, and much more. I could hardly wait to cook for him!

That evening I served him his first GF/CF meal of chicken nuggets, brown rice and corn. Much to my surprise, he tasted it, and pushed the plate away! I then added a few drops of ketchup to his chicken, but he still would not eat it. So I bit one of the chicken nuggets. It tasted awful! It was amazing that he didn't throw them! I agreed with him, but I also remembered how much money I'd just spent on these foods. They were priced much higher than regular foods! So I made him a peanut butter sandwich, sliced some apples, and looked forward to breakfast.

The next morning when he woke up, I had a plate of waffles and syrup, sausage, and scrambled eggs waiting for him. I watched him as he sat at the table. He picked up the waffle and smelled it. He then picked up the sausage and smelled it. Finally, he put his head to his plate and smelled the eggs. I'm sure you know that I was wondering, "What is he doing?" He then began to eat his food. When he finished, the sausage, and some of the waffle was still on his plate. Once again, I picked it up and tasted what he refused to eat. Yes, it was very different food! The waffle tasted like cardboard, and the sausage was bland. As the week went on, I noticed that he was not caring for many of the foods that I purchased. In fact, he was becoming a very picky eater! It was becoming more of a challenge with every meal! I was more concerned about his health, and not so much the cost of the food. I knew that it was time to call for help, so I called Dr. Buckley.

I quickly learned that the best GF/CF meals were those that were homemade, as in my learning how to make nearly everything he would eat. I was told about a GF/CF support group that met every first Tuesday of the month at one of the churches in Ponte Vedra. There I could learn more about the diet, find out what has worked for other moms, get some recipes, and sometimes even sample foods. She also gave me the names of two of the mothers who attend the group.

I attended the next meeting, and became a regular attendee. It was so comforting to be around other parents who were in this fight with me. It was easy to detect that they had been around Dr. Buckley. They too were tenacious, energetic and optimistic about their child's future. One mom had several children who were autistic. She lived an hour away, yet always attended the meetings. It was also great to see the dads that came out.

There was so much to learn about the GF/CF diet. I was an eager mom, so it didn't take long for me to learn to read food labels and ingredients, neither to understand the good stuff versus the bad stuff, such as which ketchup was GF/CF, or which foods were processed in a dedicated GF/CF facility. Even to shop at regular supermarkets again, and eat GF/CF at restaurants.

Information was available about GF/CF websites at which foods could be purchased. This was especially good for those who wanted to purchase items that were not sold in the stores. I also took home recipes from every meeting and tried them out on Daniel. He especially liked the chicken nuggets! I wonder why? (Laughs)

It eventually became second nature for me to cook GF/CF foods. The key, was using the right combination of spices, otherwise spaghetti with ground turkey could taste like punishment. I eventually weaned my entire family off of many of the foods that we were eating, and replaced them with GF/CF foods, and healthier choices. Many of the changes were simple. For example, we chose brown rice instead of white rice. Ground turkey instead of ground beef. My grilled turkey burgers could contend with any of the fast food restaurants! My other children enjoyed taking their lunch to school because of the variety of meals that I learned to prepare. We all benefited from the "diet!"

A few weeks later we went back to the doctor to find out the test results. As I sat there looking at Dr. Buckley reading the lab report, I was trying to interpret her body language so that I would not be overwhelmed by what she would say. I really didn't know what to expect, except for an answer. "Either yes, there's mercury, or no there's no mercury." Well, finally I heard the answer when she said, "This is staggering! My goodness! Poor little guy, he must be miserable!" She then showed me the lab report, and carefully explained what each column indicated. I attentively read along with her. It wasn't too complicated to comprehend. When she pointed to the column that indicated whether or not there was mercury in his body, I cried. We both sat there for a moment in disbelief. The levels were extremely high! She then said that, "It was amazing that he was able to function at all, and that treatment must begin immediately, to draw the mercury and heavy metals from his body.

We were given several different supplements to take home to begin the process. The supplements would work well along with the GF/CF diet, to naturally rid the body of the mercury and heavy metals that were leaking into his gut. Included in the supplements was a multivitamin and probiotic. I don't remember the name of the others.

I could hardly wait for the next day, to begin giving the supplements to Daniel. I was ready to have my little boy back! So on the next morning, I prepared his breakfast, and afterwards gave him his first dose back to good health: The multi-vitamin. It was a fruity – flavored chewable, and he ate it like it was candy. I then opened up the first capsule and gave it to him on a spoon. At first he cooperated because he probably thought that another fruity-flavored one was coming. But after he tasted it, he closed his lips tight, and the war began! I then tasted it and wanted to spit it out, because it was bitter and powdery, but I was not about to let him see me do it. I was convinced that the taste of it is why the pharmaceutical company put it in a capsule. It could make a grown man gag! The directions did not tell me to open the capsule, however I knew that he would not be able to swallow it. We tried it before and he always ended up with the capsule still in his mouth after swallowing the water. And I certainly did not want him to choke on it. While taking care of him, I was also trying to get rid of the after taste that was still in my mouth. I decided to drink some grape juice, and quickly realized that it might work for him too. So I put the juice on a spoon, and poured the supplement in the juice, stirred it a little, and gave it to him. He wasn't altogether sold on the idea, but cooperated, because he could sip the juice from off of the spoon. And I was relieved that the supplement was swallowed with it!

When we finished the seventh one, I did a victory dance! I was very excited, and knew that we were certainly moving forward. Now all I had to do was to repeat this, one more time, later that day, since the supplements were to be given two times a day. When it was time, he saw the juice and the whole process went much smoother than before. I was relieved, and closed my pharmacy for the day.

The next morning was day two of the road to recovery for Daniel. We had another successful day of taking supplements! I was enjoying the feeling of knowing that his body was receiving the antidote needed to restore him back to good health. He was unusually quiet, and very content watching educational DVDs. He was about the same at dinner time. Quiet. I attributed it to the supplements.

On the morning of day three, I heard him moving about in his bed, as if he was tossing and turning, so I walked over to him. His toddler bed was in our room, so that we could be near him at all times, because of his symptoms.

I gently touched him and called his name. He squirmed but didn't wake up. I tried it again. This time he woke up! He laid there for a second and just stared at me as if he was trying to focus. I knelt down next to him, lifted his hand and held it. And then he began to cry. Totally unexpected, and without any warning, not a whiny, "I'm not ready to get up!" cry, but what I call a 'real' cry. I sat on the bed to pick him up and hold him in my arms but he pulled away from me. As I asked him over and again, "What's wrong sweetheart?" he cried even more. I felt his forehead to see if he had a fever. He didn't. I checked to see if his pull-up needed to be removed. It was fine. I then went to the kitchen to get him a drink while trying to figure out what could be wrong with him. He accepted the drink, and stopped crying long enough to finish it. After he finished it, he began to cry again. As I reached for some crackers he let out a scream that scared me! I was trying everything I could think of until that last scream!

I picked up the phone and called Dr. Buckley's office. I needed someone to help me through this, and possibly tell me what was wrong. Thankfully she answered the physician's line! I explained Daniel's behavior to her, and that although I was used to him crying and screaming to communicate, this time it was different. He had never started the day this way!

She asked me, "When did you start him on the supplements, and how many of them have you given him? I replied that, "I began giving them to him two days earlier, all seven supplements, twice a day as directed." I also mentioned that, "I was opening the non-chewable capsules and putting the powder on a spoon with a small amount of grape juice to help him swallow. She then suggested that, I stop giving him the supplements for a few days. Then start over with only one supplement, and add a second, one week later, and continue until he is taking all of them again." She also stated that, "If there is an allergic reaction to any of them, it would be easier this way to determine which one. She was absolutely correct! Daniel had an allergic reaction to several of them. He continued taking only three of them.

It wasn't long before we began to see an improvement in his behavior, as well as his physique. He was a little guy, but had a noticeably large "gut." I was assured that the large gut would eventually decrease, as he continued on the supplements and the GF/CF diet. And it did.

Over the next several weeks, I was amazed at the big improvements Daniel made!

Just a Test

Amidst the excitement of Daniel's progress, a suggestion was made to enroll him in school at an early age, to give him a head start. However, the idea of our entrusting him into the care of total strangers was overwhelming. Although he no longer screamed and cried, he still was not able to verbally communicate. He wouldn't be able to tell me if someone hit him, or was mean to him. If he became ill or was hurt, he would not have been able to tell his teacher. And lastly, if someone violated him, he certainly would not have been able to say so. So, I tried to delay the process by reminding myself that neither of my two older children went to pre-kindergarten. Their first day of school was for the regular kindergarten class.

I remember sharing my concerns with a friend of mine named Natalie. She was the owner of two reputable child care centers, and acquainted with several special needs children. She referred me to our local school board district to have Daniel tested. The testing process would detect his strengths and weaknesses, and ensure him being placed in the right classroom to get the extra help he needed. The entire testing process would prove to be a learning experience to me since I was not at all familiar with what it entailed. Nevertheless, at her trusted counsel, I called and scheduled an appointment.

On the evening before the appointment, I made sure that Daniel was in bed at his usual time of eight o'clock. I wanted him to be well rested so that he would be able to endure the process. I did not want a short attention span due to sleep deprivation.

We arrived a few minutes early for the appointment. After signing him in, an administrator came out to greet us. She was ready to take Daniel to the testing area, and have me wait for him to return. But I told her that, "I would need to be with him, and further explained that he was only use to being alone with either me or my husband." She then explained that, "He would be given a variety of tests occurring on various days and locations, and that I could remain in the room if I promised to be quiet." I promised!

I kept my promise, but stretched my eyes in disbelief at different times during the tests! I was amazed by the fact that he could not follow some of the simplest commands, or answer age-appropriate questions. I watched him struggle to draw circles and to make strokes with his pencil to copy the instructor. Instead of following her command, he had a mind of his own. Each time she made a stroke and asked him to do the same thing, he just scribbled over what she did, and eventually scribbled over the entire paper. When asked to verbally answer a question, I reminded her that, "He couldn't talk." So she chose the method of having him either point to the correct answer, or pick up the object that she was referring to. He'd not only pick up an object, but also everything else in his reach. He would ball up the paper or tear it. To add to the difficulty, he often made very loud "barking" sounds. He did it without prior warning, so it was very frightening. The situation was challenging and stressful. It was obvious that he did not understand what he was being told to do, or how to do it.

In a simple card game, although he recognized animals by name, he could not tell you which one lived on a farm. If asked to, "Point to a farm, or to what else lives on a farm," he couldn't answer correctly. Instead he'd stare off into space. When spoken to, he would not make eye contact. And if there were pictures or paintings on the walls they became distractions, which only made matters worse.

I remember the test administrator giving him several colored connecting blocks, and telling him to continue the pattern of blue and red. He pulled all of the blocks toward him and began to play with them. He even reached for the pencils and crayons. When the administrator began to take them away from him, he became agitated and irritable, and tried to get up out of his seat and leave the room.

I could tell that the administrator was becoming impatient with Daniel, so I asked, "If we could take a short break?" He and I walked the hallways for a few minutes, and then went into the ladies room. I picked him up and held him. I assured him that, "I loved him, he had a wonderful future, and that he was going to grow up and be a great and powerful man." I also told him to, "Do what the test administrator tells him to do." After a few more bear hugs and kisses on the cheeks, we returned back to the testing room.

The final test waiting for him was the coloring test. It would allow him to demonstrate his ability to color within the lines of a picture, and reveal his knowledge of recognizing colors. The picture he was given to color was of a fire engine. Of all the colors available, Daniel chose black. He began to carelessly and wildly color the picture, not regarding the lines. Black was the only color he used. It was hard to recognize the fire engine once he was finished. Finally, when asked to point to the crayon when its color was called, Daniel ignored the command, grabbed all of the crayons, rubbed them between his hands, held his head back, closed his eyes, and began to playfully drop them on the table. The Administrator began to grab the crayons as they fell on the table, and Daniel was grabbing them too. It was so unexpected and funny, that I had to tighten my lips to keep from laughing. I then realized that I was needed in the room not just for Daniel, but more so for the test administrator. I believed that had I not been in there, when the testing was over, she might have come out of the room chasing him for her wig and glasses. Thank God we were finished for the day! I can only imagine what would have happened next!

We attended the scheduled meetings and test days that followed. With each one, I realized just how much my son was deficient in areas that he should have been proficient in. To me the tests were so easy that I almost questioned the administrator, or asked if they were the actual tests used to assess his level of ability. Which made it almost unbearable to watch him struggle through them. I kept thinking to myself, "This is easy. He should know this!" However, to him it was quite a mountain to climb.

On the morning of the final meeting, I woke up a little anxious and nervous. I knew that it was the day that I would find out the results of all the tests. I realized that no matter what I believed was possible, they were going to make their final assessment according to what Daniel put on paper. I had to have a pep talk with myself on the way to the testing center. I told myself that, "This assessment is not the determining factor of greatness for my son's life, not now, nor in the future!" I silently cried for a moment, and then I put on some praise and worship music. It did exactly what it was supposed to do! It made me happy! It lifted the heaviness from my heart! I began to think about the lyrics, and they brought me hope again. I was reminded that God could help me, no matter how great my problem seemed. The singer said that, "There is nothing too hard for God!" Yes, I believed it, so I started singing with the music, and by the time I drove into the testing center's parking lot I was confident and ready to take on whatever was coming.

We were greeted by two facilitators. They each carried thick binders that included the results of their assessments. After entering the conference room, we sat at the table and they both opened their books. The first facilitator explained how the tests were graded. She referred to national percentiles, averages, and projections. She compared what skills Daniel had to those he didn't have. She stated that, "At his current age of four years, he should be saying hundreds of words per day, including engaging in conversations around him. Especially at home." She also referred to his inattentiveness, lack of coordination, poor listening skills, inability to follow simple directions, hyperactivity, and the fact that his test scores were in the low national percentile. The other facilitator chimed in by saying that, "There is no way that he will function well in a mainstream classroom, therefore he will be assigned to an ESE (Exceptional Student Education) classroom at a school that specializes in his kind of challenges." She then asked me if I was familiar with the symptoms of Autism. I responded, "Yes." She then stated that, "Based upon the test results and what they've seen, Daniel has Autism."

For a few seconds there was total silence in the room. I fought back the tears that were swelling up on the inside. My stomach felt like it was in knots. But I refused to give in to it! This was not a moment for self-pity, but a moment to speak what I knew, and even greater what I believed. Finally I broke the silence by boldly saying, "The correct medical term is Vaccine Injuries, and he has already been formally diagnosed." I went on to share with them Daniel's history of being a normal, healthy little boy until he was injured by excessive amounts of mercury in his vaccination. I also shared intimate details of how challenging the last few years of our lives had been because of it. Daniel was a totally different child, seemingly living in his own world. I told them that, "He was currently being treated by Dr. Julie Buckley, an autism specialist." I concluded my response to the test results by stating that, "I am confident he will overcome this and enjoy a wonderful, productive life." At that point, one of the facilitators looked at me and had the audacity to say, "The reports of mercury in vaccines are just controversy. It has not been proven that it causes autism." I looked her in the eyes, pointed to Daniel and said, "Here's the living proof that it does!" I was angry at her selfish, insensitive comments, and she knew it! At that point the meeting was over! As I left, I assured them that I was aware that the next step was to register him for pre-kindergarten upon receipt of the school assignment that would be mailed to me.

Next School Please

The school assignment came a few weeks after the final meeting. It was determined by our geographic location in the local school district. The first day of school was two months away, so it was in my best interest to go ahead and register Daniel. Now although at that time my two other children attended an academically successful, or "A+" public school, I was not at all familiar with the school named on the assignment. So with much curiosity, I scheduled an appointment for registration.

Over the next few days many "what ifs" crossed my mind. "What if this was not a good fit, nor the best place to enroll Daniel?" "What if the classes were not set up to teach children with his kind of symptoms?" "How old are the teachers, and do have they have experience with children who are challenged?" "Do they have a passion for teaching or is it just a paycheck?" "Will they be compassionate, or mean and abusive?" After my mental Q & A session, I decided to visit the school for a tour, unannounced.

On the day of the visit I chose to go alone. I figured that Daniel could meet his teacher closer to the beginning of the new school year. As I followed the directions to the school, I couldn't help noticing that I was entering into an area of the city that caused me to feel somewhat uneasy. So following my natural instinct I made sure that all of the car doors were locked, and my purse was on the floor behind me.

The streets that I drove on were full of pot holes. There were many old boarded up buildings, including houses. The sidewalks were hidden by knee-high grass. Ditches were on both sides of the road. The stop signs leaned, and the street signs were missing. If that wasn't enough, I had to wait at a traffic light that seemingly took forever to turn green, although I was the only one waiting on either side. For a moment I almost forgot where I was going, due to my shifting into survival mode. When I finally turned onto the street that the school was on, without thinking, I yelled out, "You've gotta be kidding me!" And when I laid eyes on the school, I cried, "No way!" The school was nestled in the middle of the slums. It looked creepy and out dated. I couldn't help but wonder what the school system was doing with all of the tax payer dollars they receive. Surely this school was due a makeover! At this point I didn't know what to expect next. Nevertheless, since I was finally there it only made sense to follow through.

I entered the main office and signed in for pre-registration. The office staff was very courteous and helpful. I was given a stack of papers on a clipboard to complete. After completing the forms, I requested a tour of the school, and to meet the principal. Let me mention here that I was considered as a "walk-in," because I did not have an official appointment scheduled for that day. However, my tour request would be honored, yet a disclaimer was added. The tour guide forewarned me that, "Things might look a little cluttered and a bit unorganized today." Remembering the drive through the neighborhood to get to the school, I assured her that, " I understood." I'd already had a taste of it!

The tour guide was the head of the autism department. She told me that she had a fifteen year old autistic daughter. Her next statement sparked a little bit of anger in me. "They never get well. They don't recover, like fixing a leaky faucet over and over." Having heard enough, I quickly responded, "That's not true. My youngest son is recovering from autism and he's making great strides!" She had another rebuttal, so I mentioned the DAN! process and told her to take a look at the Autism Research Institutes' (ARI) website for more information. I wasn't about to waste time getting into a debate with her. I was trying to find a school for my son.

Finally we were at the entrance of the Autism Department. I noticed that it was the farthest building from the main office, so I asked, "Why?" The guide explained that on the other side of the walls was the loading and unloading area for the buses. We then visited one of the classrooms. I didn't know what to expect, since I'd never been in a classroom for special needs children. So I just followed closely and observed. By the expression on the teacher's face we certainly caught her and her team by surprise. The room was dirty, smelly, and cluttered. It lacked beautiful, vibrant colors that one would expect for children. It was referred to as, "The Multipurpose," room and indoor gym, which explains why I saw a class playing kickball. None of the children seemed to notice us. Even as we walked passed them, they did not respond. It was as if we were invisible. After being introduced as a parent of a new student, the teachers seemed relieved that I was not an administrator from the school's district office.

There was this one teacher in particular who was being challenged by a little girl. When I say little, I mean that the child could not have been older than four or five. She was very defiant! She refused to follow the teacher's instructions. The teacher exercised her authority, but it turned into a power struggle. Then all of a sudden, the child took off running. Everybody who was not attending to a class ran after her, including my tour guide. It looked like a miniature race, with the child winning. I quickly walked and stood next to the nearest wall, out of their path. Once she was caught, the little girl began screaming, scratching, and kicking the teachers. There were about three adults holding her to the floor. After she calmed down, I was told that the behavior was typical for a child with autism, and assured that the teacher was well capable of handling it. The child's behavior was termed a "meltdown." Meltdowns can manifest in various behaviors, at any time, and usually without warning. They can be sparked by almost anything, However, with the proper medical treatment, the "triggers" can be revealed, and even prevented. They vary with each person. Although many children with autism have meltdowns, not all of them do. The teacher's ultimate goal is to prevent injury to the child who is having the meltdown, as well as to others in their presence.

After things were back to normal, we left the area to tour the buildings where the mainstream classes were taught. Once inside, I noticed the dull, pale blue color on the walls. The same stale odor filled the air. It made me feel gloomy. I was ready to go. So I told the guide, "You don't have to show me anymore. This is sufficient."

We returned to the main office where I met the school's principal. He was a very kind and warm-hearted man. He thanked me for visiting the school, and mentioned that he'd like for me to consider being a part of their Parent Teacher Association (PTA). I smiled and thanked him as I exited the door.

My ride home was very quiet, and full of thought. Even if the staff was doing their best, it just was not impressive enough for me to put my son there. I saw no love or passion from the teachers for the students. There were no smiles. No laughter. Only gloom and doom. I thoroughly understood the nature of the business, but c'mon, these were children. I believe if someone smiled at them, they would have smiled back. No, I didn't need to be there on another day when things might have been different. I was there on that day, and my decision would be based on it. Sounds unfair? No! Again we're talking about my little boy. My baby. And you only get one chance to make a first impression!

So, my decision was made. There was no way that I would enroll Daniel there! However my heart was still somewhat heavy after witnessing the little girl's meltdown. I couldn't help thinking about how the little girl must feel seeing she was unable to properly express herself, and also how her parents must feel. She, too, is somebody's little one, somebody's baby.

I Thank God for the Lighthouse

Feeling a little bit overwhelmed, I resorted to the fact that I made the right decision regarding the other school. There was no way that I could allow Daniel to attend there, knowing that I did not feel good about it. However, I now had to start all over, again in my pursuit of finding the right school for him. I didn't know where to start. At the time, I was not familiar with the numerous agencies that provided assistance to families of special needs children. So I chose to look in the local telephone directory, in hope of finding a lead to the perfect match.

At the end of the first week, I'd had very little success. There were numerous public and private schools, even state-of-the-art child care centers, but none of them accepted children with autism. As a result, I was becoming very discouraged because I'd exhausted all of my leads. As I began to meditate on the desire to find the right school, I couldn't help asking myself, "Are you telling me that there are no schools or centers in Jacksonville that cater to autism?" "If there are, where would they most likely be located, and why aren't they listed in the telephone directory?" I sat silently for a few minutes, trying to imagine what the right center would look like, and what other businesses might be in its vicinity: hospitals, physician offices, labs, other schools, etc. Then all of a sudden it happened! The most wonderful thought came to my mind, "Since I couldn't find a facility in my county, search in the other counties!" Wow! Why hadn't I thought of that before? Although I lived in the Duval County school district, there were three other adjacent districts to the Jacksonville area, including the one that Dr. Buckley practiced in. They were all within minutes from where I lived. Brilliant! Hallelujah! And to keep this idea equally simple, and sensible, I immediately made a decision to start looking in the one closest to me, Clay County.

My work was "cut-out." But I had a plan! On the following Monday morning I excitedly took out the telephone directory again. I made phone call after phone call to the different child care centers. I wasn't bothered by the, "No's," because I knew that I had several options, and I had just begun! Most of the centers were extremely busy at the time of my call, so they just answered my question as to whether or not they cared for children with autism. Although I would ask to speak to the Director, most of my conversations were with whichever employee answered the phone. During the course of one of the conversations, I was asked if I'd called The Lighthouse Center for Children. Of course I hadn't, so I was very eager to know more about it. I was told that it was a facility specifically for children with special needs, and not only included a daycare and school, but also rehabilitation. To this day, I do not remember who gave me this tip, but I took their advice, called the center and scheduled a tour.

I called my husband at work and shared the news! Knowing that we'd been praying for the right place, I couldn't help but to believe again. I had to let go of the memory of the other school, and be prepared to tour this one with an open mind. I also called Dr. Buckley and told her about the center, and asked if she was familiar with it. She said that, "She had heard of it, and looked forward to my sharing with her after the tour."

On the morning of the tour, I arrived at the center a few minutes early. It gave me a few extra minutes to relax, but also to observe the surroundings. It was located in both a business and residential area. The community looked productive and fruitful. There were no boarded up windows on buildings, nor sidewalks covered with knee-high grass. Doctor's offices, restaurants, and even a library were in walking distance. The streets were wide and well maintained. No potholes. Lastly, I noticed that there was an eight foot high iron, cemented fence that surrounded the center's playground. The children could see through the fence, but they couldn't get out. Neither could an outsider get in.

Finally, it was time for the appointment. I entered the building and stepped inside a small lobby. It was as far as I could go. I could see the inside of the center. There were children being pulled in a large, red wagon. Others were walking in a line on their way to the lunchroom. The teachers spoke as they past one another. But no one took notice of me until I rang the bell at the security window. The receptionist opened the window, greeted me, and asked, "How may I help you?" I told her my name and that I was there for a scheduled tour. Entrance into the tinted glass door could only be granted by my signing in, showing a valid picture I.D., and being approved by her.

Access was granted, and I was taken to a conference room where I was greeted by the center's director. She was very kind, and her welcome was heartfelt. We sat and had a general discussion regarding Daniel's autism diagnosis. I was pleased to know that although she did not know a lot about vaccine injuries, she'd at least heard of several cases in which vaccine injuries produced the onset of autism, and she wanted to learn more about it. She assured me that they provided all of the services that he would need, including therapies. She also reminded me that, "Autism Spectrum Disorder (ASD) is referred to as such, because it covers a wide range of symptoms, and varies from child to child." As a result of this, they housed the healthcare providers most commonly needed: Speech and Language, Occupational, Physical, and Behavioral Therapists. I then took the liberty to share with her the current treatment that Daniel was receiving, and the tremendous progress he'd made. I referred to Dr. Buckley as his specialist, and how her treatments put him on the road to recovery. After the conversation we went on the tour.

The center was nearly five times the size of what it appeared to be from the outside looking in. There were all kinds of classrooms, therapy rooms, and play areas. The hallways were extremely wide to allow the children in wheelchairs to have fun as well. Each classroom had at least two teachers. Almost all of the children enrolled were being treated for an exceptionality, yet there were a small handful of others who did not have a special need, but were just there for pre-kindergarten.

Along the tour we occasionally stopped to greet administrators and other staff members that we saw in the hallway. I was briefly introduced to them as we crossed paths. We continued on to the lunchroom, and after meeting the manager and discussing Daniel's dietary needs, we headed to the class for children with autism.

As we approached the class I was warned that it was one of the most challenging classes in the school, due to behavioral problems associated with autism. The students' conditions ranged from low to high on the spectrum. As a result of the numerous conditions, we would see various protective gear throughout the classroom, such as helmets to protect the students who bang their heads against the wall. I assured her that I would be fine no matter what I saw. However, deep inside I knew that it would not take much for me to cry in the presence of these precious little ones, especially since I was all too familiar with some of the behaviors that were described, but I chose to be strong. I remember one instance when I was playing with Daniel, and decided to pretend that I was crying, it triggered his emotions, and he began to cry uncontrollably. It startled me, because I had not seen that behavior in him before. So after consoling him and apologizing, I realized that I couldn't play with him like that anymore. The autism had really heightened his sensitivity.

We entered the classroom without any prior notice. The teachers were fully engaged assisting two or more children at a time. They said, "Hello," and continued working. The children were very active. It was a loud and busy environment. There were constant sounds of barking, crying, and screams. Objects were quickly taken from little hands to prevent them from being thrown at another student. Some students ran through the classroom, while others literally sat and stared into space, a look that I was all too familiar with. And just as I was forewarned, there were three children who wore helmets. Nevertheless, despite the seemingly chaotic environment, I carefully took note of how well the teachers handled each situation. They remained calm, but responded quickly where needed. They didn't seem stressed or frazzled, although they certainly had every reason to be. The administrator briefly spoke to them about my enrolling my son who had autism. The teachers responded that, "They looked forward to meeting him." I felt a sense of sincerity from them. They displayed genuine love and compassion for the students. They were patient.

Realizing that the tour was over, just before we turned onto the hallway leading back to the conference room, I asked if I could visit the general education classroom for the four year olds in pre-kindergarten. Without hesitation my request was granted. When we opened the classroom door, the students were sitting in a circle on a large yellow and red rug. They hardly noticed that we entered the room because they were captured by the story their teacher was reading to them. The administrator shared with me that the children's ages range from three to five. She also stated that although some students were not as vocal as others, the class remained progressive, with most of the five year olds graduating and continuing on to kindergarten at the end of the school year. The daily class schedule was structured, and provided a good balance of academics and fun. The administration had proven that only four hours per day was enough schooling for a pre-kindergartener. My visit was an enjoyable one, well received.

Upon returning to the conference room, the administrator wasted no time asking my opinion. Her first question was, "Well, what do you think?" Followed by, "Do you think we're a good fit for Daniel?" My response was simple. "Yes, I like what I've seen here. I feel good about it, and would like to enroll him." We then took a look at the results of his assessment tests on his Individual Education

Plan (IEP). Afterwards, she made a recommendation to enroll him in the autism classroom. There was only one space available and she gladly offered it to him.

Now considering the fact that I visited both the autism and pre-kindergarten class, I knew that Daniel would not thrive in the wild and aggressive environment of the autism classroom. He would have been terrified. Furthermore, the behavior issues and other quirky behaviors seen were obstacles he'd overcome. He had not been in that type of environment since he began to come out of the "window." So I shared my view with her and requested that Daniel be enrolled in the pre-kindergarten class. She then reminded me that he couldn't talk. I responded that although he didn't have much language, he did have some, and he was constantly progressing. Therefore, it would benefit him to be in the class with children who are talking so that he will have something to reach for.

With that exchange of views, she ended the conversation by saying, "Mrs. Christie, I don't usually do what I'm about to do. We assign our students to a class based upon the written documentation and test scores provided to us by the school district. We realize that it can be difficult for a parent to accept that their child has special needs, and require to be in a self-contained classroom. However, based upon what you've shared with me regarding your son's vaccine injury diagnosis, the fact that he's being treated by an autism specialist, and most important of all that he does not have behavior issues, I am going to enroll him in our pre-kindergarten class. He can begin on next Monday at nine. I'll inform the teachers that he's coming".

I completed and signed the enrollment forms, agreed to the school's rules, confirmed that I would send a GF/CF lunch and snack every day, received my copies, shook hands, and walked out of the door smiling from ear to ear! Ecstatic!!!

Only heaven knows how I reached the destination of my car. Did I walk or float? Any how, I remained calm until I was completely out of sight from the school. I didn't want them to see how crazy I was about to act!

Finally, I'd driven far enough! I let the lid off of my suppressed scream, clapped my hands, yelled, and told the Lord, "Thank you" over and over and over until I was nearly exhausted! I didn't care who saw me. I was even willing to risk being stopped by the police. I think they would have loved my story! Don't you?

After my celebration, I sobered up enough to complete the drive home and share the good news with my husband. Yahoo!!!!

On the Roll

"Daniel Christie?" "Here!" No, he couldn't say it yet, but as I stood quietly with the other parents behind the tinted windows of the observation room, I said it for him. "Here!" He was finally in school! All of my hours of tedious research and hard work had paid off!

It was his first day of school at "The Lighthouse" and another exciting step on the path to recovery. I talked to him during the drive there, assuring him that he would have lots of fun learning, and that he would make new friends, and have fun with his teachers. Most of all, I wanted him to know that mommy would be there to pick him up when school was over.

Call me a bag of water if you wish, because I cried all the way home. I missed him the moment I walked out of the school without him. The staff had made it very easy for me to "let go," by allowing me to stand inside of the observation room as long as I wanted to. The two rooms were connected, and I could have stayed there all day, but I knew I had to learn to drop him off, and leave. So twenty minutes after the school day began, I finally left.

As expected, Daniel had an outstanding first day of school! His teachers gave me a good report about it. They also noted that although he didn't talk much, he got along well with the other children, and followed directions. It wasn't hard for him to find his way around the classroom. And like most kids, he had to learn to share the toys, particularly the books.

As excited as I was, I was all the more excited for him to begin therapy. What a relief to know that he would begin tackling the language deficit. Although we had quite a way to go, I couldn't help imagining him holding a conversation with me again. Yes, I was seeing the end result even before we started. But isn't that what hope gives to us, an expectation?

The therapy room was very similar to the classroom, in that it also had an observation room connected to it. I stayed in the room with Daniel and the therapist for the first three sessions. However, just to make sure that I wasn't being a distraction to him, I began observing from the adjacent room. Much to my surprise, he took advantage of my absence in his session. He misbehaved and clowned around with the therapist. I watched in disbelief as he purposely did the opposite of what she instructed him to do. He even smiled as he ran from one side of the room to the next, picking up stuffed animals and ignoring her as she called him over and again. I found myself laughing. He was absolutely hilarious, having himself a good time while she was becoming more and more frustrated. Had she stood up and began to chase him I would have lost what little composure I had left. I knew I had to step in to save her. Furthermore, she knew that I was on the other side of the dark glass observing it all. So I wiped the smile off of my face and went back into their room. Daniel immediately stopped clowning when he saw me, and dropped the stuffed animals. I had to swallow a few times to keep from laughing. I took the time to correct him, and reminded him to obey the rules. The therapist nodded in agreement as if she was doing the talking. At the end of the session, he collected the stuffed animals and other toys from all four corners of the room and neatly put them away. The session was finally over and we headed home. During the drive home,, I had a flashback of the entire event and began laughing again. You know, their performance could have won at least $10,000 on America's Funniest Videos (AFV)! No doubt.

By the end of the school year Daniel had gone through three speech therapists. He was a pretty tough cookie, and considering his autism diagnosis, they probably felt limited in regards to correcting his behavior. However, the last therapist had a survival plan! She made a keen discovery that it was not a good idea for Daniel to leave his class and immediately go to therapy. The little guy needed a break, with a snack at that! So after she discovered the missing element, it was smooth sailing from that moment on. She gave him a break, and he gave her one in return!

The plan was working! The GF/CF diet, supplements, speech therapy, school, home. It was all coming together, and we were beginning to see even greater progress in Daniel's overall development. He even began to use language that we could understand. Nearly every day after school he would bring a book to us, and say, "Read!" Then he'd sit on the floor as if he was in his reading circle at school. The excitement of hearing the story made him flap his arms and make loud noises. Sometimes he'd point to the previously read page so that I could read it again. If he really liked it, we'd read it again and again.

Week after week Daniel enjoyed his academic journey. The school's partnership with us was slowly but surely moving him ahead. I remember the day he came home saying the names of his classmates. He initially named only the two he sat in between, and eventually the entire class. Every day on our way home, I'd ask him if he had a good day. He'd answer, "Yes." Once we were home and relaxed, I'd sit him on my lap, and while cuddling, we'd discuss more of his school day: The questions went something like this: "Did you make a new friend today?" "Did your table share the coloring books and crayons?" "How about the toys and reading books?" "Did you eat all of your lunch?" "Did anyone ask for or try to take some of your food?" His answers were always short and straight to the point. So I'd continue our Q & A session: "Was it fun playing on the playground today?" "Were you all nice and kind to one another?" "Ok, who was sent to timeout?" " Was anyone mean to you?" "Were you mean to anyone? "Did anybody hit you?" Did anybody try to kiss you on the lips or touch your private parts?

There was no official list of questions. I just followed my heart. Neither did the fact that Daniel was dealing with a disability prompt or motivate me. Instead it was simply due to having a child in school. My two older children were asked very similar questions in their early years. And even today at the ages of 14, 12, and 10, being involved in extracurricular activities at school and in the community, we still have Q & A sessions. Why? Because I want to know what's going on with my children. Is there a fear that something bad will happen? No. As a parent it's my responsibility to my children and to God. It also teaches them what is acceptable, and unacceptable, how well they are to be treated, and encourages conversation from them.

During his inaugural year of schooling, Daniel was a sponge. Such a quest for knowledge! It wasn't enough for him to complete his homework assignments and be done. He always wanted more. Can you imagine not having to wrestle to get homework done, and in addition, to be asked for more? Well this was the beginning of what would be the norm for him. It required me to supplement with more books and letter writing paper. It was also during this time, that he acquired an interest for computers. I thought it was cute for him to sit next to whoever was on the computer and watch, while they played games. I had no idea that he was really paying attention, until his teacher brought it to my attention.

On one particular afternoon, Ms. Tina approached me with a humorous conversation about Daniel: "Who taught Daniel how to use the computer?" "I wasn't aware that he knew how to use one," I responded. "Well he does," she said. "For the past few days we've been trying to figure out which teacher keep leaving on the computer after using it. Everybody has denied leaving it on, yet everyday we've noticed that it is not only left on, but also one of the kiddie discs that we use is inserted. "Finally today during the transition from writing, to moving over to the reading rug, we noticed that as the children were putting away their pencils and crayons and moving throughout the room, Daniel purposely walked near the computer. He pushed the "on" button, quickly popped in a disc, and then ran over to the reading area as if nothing happened." We laughed in disbelief watching him, someone so little appearing to know what they were doing. And at the same time relieved to finally know who was responsible. So, from that moment we decided to keep the computer cabinet locked until we needed to use it." I assured her that I would remind Daniel that the computer could be used only by permission, and that otherwise he is not to touch it.

Following that conversation, I knew that at home we had to encourage Daniel's desire to use the computer. So, we did just that. We purchased age-appropriate educational CDs that included matching letters, recognizing numbers, counting, and even coloring. My husband and I would take turns sitting with him while he learned how to use the programs. Let me remind you that at this time Daniel was still building language skills. He was not a fluent speaker yet. But just by observing us, he was able to grasp how to use a computer. Totally Awesome!

The one quality I really appreciated about this school was the fact that although most of the children had an obvious disability, they were still given opportunities and memorable experiences, not to mention the best possible care and education. It was not a watered-down, daycare-type school that was full of unhappy, screaming kids. Nor of educators who were angry and abusive. But it was a peaceful and loving haven. The ambiance of love was so warm, that it rested upon you like a blanket. The children knew that those caring for them enjoyed it. And it was also evident to the parents.

One of my most memorable experiences is the field trip to the pumpkin patch, during harvest time in October. I volunteered to be one of the chaperones, and the day finally arrived! Nearly every class in the school was going on the field trip, including those in the autism area and in wheelchairs. The pumpkin patch was approximately three blocks from the school. But we had to cross a major intersection in order to get there. The distance of the pumpkin patch was not my main concern. My concern was the means of transportation to transport the number of students going on the field trip, and how were we going to cross that busy intersection. Realizing that a permission slip to ride a bus was not sent home, I asked Ms. Tina, "How are we being transported?" When she responded, "Oh we're walking, " I thought that it was a bad joke. But she was not joking. When her class reached the parking lot, there were several classes already in line. I struggled to keep my mouth from dropping open at the sight of the means of transportation. The school had provided giant stroller-like "rides." Each ride could seat up to eight students, and included a child-proof seatbelt. Most of the occupants were the autistic children who were prone to run away from their teacher. Not only did the teachers and parents attend the fieldtrip, but there were also nurses and therapists. There was a multitude of people in the parking lot, and oh so orderly!

That autumn day was absolutely beautiful. The weather was perfect. Not too cold, not too hot. The walk was a nice stroll filled with conversation and laughter. Ms. Tina's class asked many questions along the way. My attention was present; however it was being distracted with every step closer to that major intersection. Then without warning the unthinkable happened! Just about the time the front of the group was near the intersection, a police car came racing past us with its lights flashing. I immediately felt a sense of danger. It certainly was not the time for a police chase, not with all of the children around. And I knew that screaming could have caused chaos. So I remained calm, and kept my eyes on the speeding police car. At about the time it should have turned at the intersection, it did something totally unexpected. It stopped in the middle of the intersection! And immediately the police officer got out and told the group to stop. No one seemed alarmed but me. They simply followed his command. I, on the other hand, thought that he was going to give the school a citation for taking so many disabled children on a major road. Little did I know that he was a part of the fieldtrip. He had arrived at his post on schedule and after closing his door, blew his whistle and stopped all of the traffic in order to allow us to cross over to the other side. I was dumbfounded! Later I couldn't help thinking that we must have looked like Moses and the Children of Israel crossing the Red Sea.

We went on to have an outstanding day at the pumpkin patch, and on the way back to the school the same police officer was promptly on his post to stop traffic ,so that we could safely cross to the other side. Needless to say, I fell in love with the school that day, and sought ways for Daniel to remain there throughout his elementary school years. What a heartbreak it was to learn that the curriculum was only through pre-kindergarten, meaning that he would graduate at the end of the current school year.

As we approached the end of the school year, a greater focus was placed on potty training Daniel. It was unsuccessful. Each time he was taken for a potty break, he had already soiled his pull-up. On the other hand, because he was there for only four hours per day, he was able to master holding his bowels until he reached home. It went without explanation. However, Dr. Buckley assured me that when he was ready to, he would master potty training, but in the meantime, continue to sit him on the potty, and give him lots of encouragement.

During the final semester of the school year, Ms. Tina approached me and commended me on teaching Daniel to become such an avid reader. She questioned how much time we were spending with him each evening, and if we were using any special reading programs. I responded in amazement and told her that, "We've noticed for weeks how he not only loves books, but is also now reading. However, we could not take the credit. We thought that she and Ms. Helen were teaching him to read." She responded that, "They do spend time reading with the students, but not one on one, and that he was already reading on a kindergarten level." I told her, "If you all are not teaching him, and neither are we, then it has to be another miracle." And miracle it was. Daniel's love for books increased. He really loves to read.

The school year ended with the pre-kindergarten graduation. Each student was to make a presentation to the audience by displaying their talent, or sharing something they learned during the school year. Before we had a chance to suggest what Daniel would do, Ms.

Tina approached us and said that, "I have the perfect presentation for Daniel. The audience will absolutely enjoy him reading a book to them. So dress him up in a shirt and tie, and I will set a small rocking chair in the front center of the stage, lower the lights in the auditorium, and he will read to the audience." We thought it was a wonderful idea, and agreed to it.

I put an extra tissue in my purse on the night of the graduation. Considering all that Daniel had been through and was still dealing with, I just knew that it would be an emotional event for me. Certainly it would have been understandable for me or for any of the parents to cry. It was a joyous occasion. A once in a lifetime event. But much to my surprise, I didn't shed a tear. At the sound of the music, the audience stood as the first graduate marched, trying to step in time with the music. After reaching the fifth seat, the next graduate entered, and so on. Finally, stepping in alphabetical order at number four, Daniel marched in looking straight ahead. We called out his name but he would not turn his head. The look on his face was serious. He was focused on Ms. Tina, who was giving directions with her hand. He looked like a little college chancellor. He remained in that disposition until he walked across the stage to receive his diploma. As he exited the stage he ran down the steps, and leaped from the second one to the floor. Every one after him did the same thing. The audience roared with laughter, as the teachers tried to stop the next student from repeating this behavior. They were momentarily successful.

The individual student presentations would be the finale for the evening. They included singing duets, trios, poem recitations, speeches, and yes, the book reading. The presentations were best described as entertainment. From the seat, to the stage, and back to the seat, the students clowned and giggled as they made their presentation. And as they exited the stage, you guessed it. They jumped from that second step to the floor, both the boys and the girls. We laughed over and again. Finally, a small rocking chair was placed front and center on the stage. We heard what sounded like someone stomping up the steps onto the stage. Well, that's exactly what it was. Daniel came up the stairs with much noise. He ran to his rocking chair, and by the time he sat down, his shirt was partly out of his pants, and his tie was off-centered. We couldn't stop laughing. Then, for the first time that evening, he looked in our direction and when he saw us laughing, he started laughing too. I managed for a quick second to make a stern face at him while telling him to stop, only to join in with the audience's laughter again. The audience soon quieted down, so that he could be heard. He then began to read, "My New School." He did a wonderful job reading to us. As he was nearing the end of the book two teachers went and stood at either side of the stage. When he finished reading, he quickly said, "The End!" Then jumped up out of the chair, ran across the stage to the stairs and looked into the eyes of the teacher as the lights came up. He stopped in his tracks, walked down each step to the floor, then took off running to his seat. Laughter and clapping arose from the audience once again, because he walked only long enough to get past the teacher. I never had a chance to cry tears of sorrow on that night, because the children kept me laughing! What a stellar school year it was!

Tug of War

With the school year now ended, we were well into the summer break. It indeed was a break, but I also knew I had to register Daniel for kindergarten. There was only one school that The Lighthouse recommended ----Tyndale Elementary. It was the most reputable school in North Florida and South Georgia for students on the autism spectrum. It was also the only school where The Lighthouses' students were assigned after completing pre-kindergarten. So without question I settled it in my heart that he would attend Tyndale Elementary.

Now if there was one tough lesson I learned on Daniel's journey, it was the fact that not everyone was as excited about his recovery as I. The attitude of some of the professionals depicted that because they'd seen so many autistic children, if they'd seen one, they'd seen them all. These responses surprised me the most when they came from professionals of the public school system's Special Education Department.

On one particular morning I called Tyndale Elementary School and spoke with the principal. I shared Daniel's story with her, and how that Tyndale came highly recommended for his continual academic progress. I requested information to enroll him there. She questioned which subdivision we lived in, and asked for our home address, so I told her the address, confident that it would not pose a problem. However, without any warning or tact, she firmly responded, "I am not accepting out of district students. We're already overcrowded!" I then asked her if she would reconsider since he was transferring from The Lighthouse. She again denied my request, adding sternness to her voice. Rude. At that point there was no need to continue the conversation. The assertive side of me would normally have pursued my request, but I could feel anger slowly rising in me, so I thanked her and hung up the phone. I then called the school district's main office and requested the Exceptional Student Education (ESE) office.

Mr. Burke answered the call. I shared Daniel's wonderful story with him, including his outstanding, inaugural year of kindergarten at The Lighthouse. I went on to say that, " I would like for Daniel to continue his education in the Clay County school district. "Where do you live?" He asked. After I told him, he laughed and said, "No, he can't stay in this district! We're already overcrowded! As a matter of fact, I'm the district police who makes sure kids like yours don't get in!" It sounded like a bad joke, so in return I asked, " Are you kidding me?" He answered, "No, I'm not kidding you. Unless you live in this school district, you will have to find another school for your son. We just can't let everyone in. Sure I understand your request, and I'm happy to hear about your son's progress, but the answer is still, no." Only for peace sake did I allow that comment to be the end of the conversation.

I spent the next few days making phone calls to the schools district office in my area. They gave me a list of prospects. I scheduled appointments and went on more tours. I was very impressed with three schools in particular. Although it would require a thirty minute drive one way, I was willing to sign off on any of the three. The principals at two of the schools were very cordial, and looked forward to Daniel's tentative enrollment. However, my experience with the principal at the third school was not good. She was very uncooperative. She advised me that, "She would not grant him enrollment due to the possibility of a higher volume of new enrollees that live in her school's geographical area." I told her that, "I only needed to enroll one child and that I know she has the space for him because the school district referred me to her!" She was speechless. She then quickly walked towards her office and without looking back at me said, "I'm not going to do it!" A part of me wanted to follow her into the office and really give her a piece of my mind, but I knew that it would have escalated into something undesirable, such as her calling the police and accusing me of harassment! So I shouted loud enough for her to hear me, "I'm leaving here and going directly downtown to the school district office, and whatever paperwork I have to complete, know that I am filing a formal complaint, and it will not just go to the district office! No parent should have to deal with this kind of nonsense!"

I cried on my way to the school district office. I was very angry and needed to calm down. I was also tired of this entire autism ordeal. I wanted my life to be normal. I wanted Daniel to be normal. I was exhausted from having to find another school. I didn't expect to have to do this again after finding The Lighthouse. It was supposed to be the path that led to all of the great schools that would follow his enrollment there. But that's not what was happening on this day. To top it all off, I felt like I was in this alone. Although I shared information with my family, no one could really identify what I personally was going through. No, not even my husband. Yes, he listened when I shared stories or doctor's visit results. But many times he would say, "Sheila I'm sorry, this is just so much information." This was usually my cue to stop talking about it. My support group was forty-five minutes from my house, and we only met on Tuesday nights. I hadn't exchanged phone numbers with anyone in the support group because I was so busy trying to learn what information I could about autism.

By the time I reached the school district office I felt a little better because of the release that came from crying, I also prayed and asked the Lord for his help again. Once inside the special needs office I was able to speak to an administrator and share my dilemma, including my experience with the last school principal. At the end of our conversation I completed several forms including the submission of my top three school choices. I left there feeling a sense of accomplishment. I would now need to allow two to three weeks for a formal response and school assignment in writing. It would be delivered by mail.

With the beginning of the new school year fastly approaching, there was much to do while waiting for the school assignment. The days that followed were full of preparation for all three of my children. Not to mention gearing up for our annual end of the summer weekend trip. So I became as busy as a bee!

After two and one half weeks passed, I began to pay close attention to the mail. Finally towards the mark of week three the school assignment came in the mail. With great anticipation I read the letter to learn which school was our new school. I quickly discovered that the letter did not provide that information. Instead, it was a notification that the school district denied all three of my requests on the basis that the schools I chose were in anticipation of a higher volume of new enrollments for the new school year. And their suggestion, are you ready for this, was for Daniel to attend his original school assignment----Pinehill Elementary. I screamed out loud, "Nooooo! Not in a million years!" If you recall, Pinehill was the school that we ran from before we found The Lighthouse.

At this point I could feel my emotions intensifying. I was beyond angry! I was absolutely ticked off! I immediately called the district's special needs office and requested to speak to the administrator who assisted me three weeks earlier. When she came to the phone, I recalled the day that she and I spoke. Of course she remembered me. I went on to tell her that I had just received the school assignment in the mail, and the decision that was made. She responded, "Yes, it's unfortunate, but we are looking at projections for the upcoming school year. So the district made its decision based upon that." I yelled at her and said, you denied my son entry to not one, but all three schools based upon a projection?! That's not fair! I spent over an hour talking to you about my son, and the challenge of finding him a new school. You made me think that you were concerned and wanted to help. Why would you even give me the option of other schools if you knew that you were only going to deny it? Why didn't you just tell me that the only school you would assign him to is the one in his geographical area. Lady, where's your heart?" She was quiet for a few seconds, and finally said, "Mrs. Christie I'm really sorry." I responded, "So am I. Thank you." And hung up the phone.

"Think Sheila! Think! Think! Think!" What was I to do next?! School started in exactly two weeks. It was a requirement that Daniel be enrolled from day one. There was no time to learn about home schooling. Besides, home schooling would mean that he'd miss out on most of his therapies. And I wasn't sure which ones our health insurance covered other than for speech. Furthermore, I couldn't jeopardize his progress. He'd had such an outstanding year in his pre-kindergarten class. So think. Think!"

I resorted back to the local telephone directory to review the list of other specialty schools in the area. There were two listed. One cost $25,000 annually. The other $40,000. I could care less how much they cost. I was ready to do whatever was necessary for my son. However, much to my surprise, the first one refused him because he had some language and could do basic things for himself. The second school refused him because he did well in pre-kindergarten. What? I was dumbfounded! After speaking to both schools, it appears that they had similar requirements. "They were looking for children who were totally dependent, and not able to do anything for themselves." Although Daniel had a long way to go, the little progress that he made kept him from being accepted. I was somewhat speechless. But for some reason it felt good that he was doing too well to be accepted to either school. So now what? I was back to square one. The day was far spent, and my search would have to begin again on the next day.

I woke up thinking the same thoughts that I had before I went to sleep the night before. "Where can I find a good school to enroll Daniel? Where do I even began to look?" While taking care of the children that morning, I found myself whispering to God, "Father please help me. I have visited so many schools and talked to all of the right people, but no one has accepted his enrollment. School starts in less than one month and I'm not sure where he's going. Will you please help me again? You know which school is best for him. I trust your lead. Thank you."

If there was one thing that I enjoyed along this journey, it was talking to God. I knew that I was talking to someone who was bigger than my problem. I also sensed that He was listening, and really cared enough to not just do something about it, but to make it right. And afterwards I would feel such a peace on the inside. It would literally calm me down. I knew that it was His way of responding to me.

So, immediately after making breakfast for the kids I took out our local telephone directories for what seemed like the millionth time. I began the search, conscious of school beginning in just a few weeks. While flipping through the pages of the telephone directory my eyes scanned some of the same schools that I had contacted before. It was very annoying to see them again because I was looking for businesses that I might had overlooked. But these were the "same ole' same ole'." Finally I decided to do some cold calling. These calls included banks, churches, daycares, and even private home schools. I figured since women were the primary employees at these places, they just might have had an onsite childcare facility that was also open to the public. I also was not hesitant to make my request because I knew that Daniel would do well. It was just a matter of finding the right facility, and he becoming acquainted with it.

As I continued my search that day, the weirdest thought came to my mind to call Dr. Burke at the Clay County School District. Of course I immediately remembered our last telephone conversation, which was reason enough for me to altogether dismiss the thought. But this was not about how much his remarks insulted me. In fact it was not about me at all. It was about my son. So instead of allowing those memories to upset me, I felt all the more impressed to call him. And so I did.

He answered his phone promptly. This was the telephone conversation:

Mr. Burke: *"Hello this is Mr. Burke."*

Me: *"Hi Mr. Burke, my name is Sheila Christie. My son, Daniel Christie attended The Lighthouse last school year, and on one particular day I had the pleasure of meeting you. As you know, Daniel has an autism diagnosis, however he progressed tremendously at The Lighthouse School. Therefore I would like for him to continue his education in Clay County.*

Mr. Burke: *"Oh yes, I remember Daniel. He was in Ms. Tina's class. A fine young man. How is he doing now?"*

Me: *"He's doing very well. The year that he spent at The Lighthouse was remarkable! Although he has an autism diagnosis, he was placed in the regular pre-kindergarten class, and it was a perfect match for him. As a result of it he began to talk again, learned to use the computer, and even read a book to the audience at the graduation. He'll be in the first grade in just a few weeks."*

Mr. Burke: *"That's wonderful news!" "That's the kind of report we like to hear!" "I'm so glad for you!" "Now where will he be attending school in the fall?"*

Me: *"Well, that's what I'm calling you about." "Because he did so well at The Lighthouse, I'd like for him to continue his education in The Clay county school district. The knowledge he gained is just simply outstanding, and furthermore, I was told that the most reputable school in North Florida and South Georgia for children with autism is located in Clay County. Tynedale Elementary. Tynedale was also highly recommended by the staff at The Lighthouse. They told me that it's the school where they send all of their autism students."*

Mr. Burke: *"Mrs. Christie where do you live?"*

Me: *"We live in Argyle Forest, but on the Duval County side."*

Mr. Burke: *"Well that's no problem. I'm sure we can make room for Daniel at Tyndale School. However, in order to make that happen, there are a few mandatory steps that you'll need to act upon immediately. You see Daniel will be considered as an out- of- county transfer student, therefore you'll need permission from the school Superintendent of both counties before we can enroll him."*

Me: *OK. So, what exactly do I need to do?*

Mr. Burke: *"First you'll need to write a letter to the superintendent of Duval County and request permission for Daniel to leave Duval County to attend school in Clay County. Second, you'll have to wait for their response in writing, because the third step requires a copy of their response. The third and final step is for you to write a letter to the superintendent of Clay County and request permission for Daniel to be accepted into Clay County as an out-of-county transfer student. Once the paperwork is received we can complete the process. However, at this point you're working within a very short timeframe. As you already know, the first day of school is in less than a month. It could take up to two weeks alone for Duval to receive your request, submit it to the superintendent, and afterwards send you a response. Then it could take another week or two for the same process here in Clay County. I'm not saying that it can't be done in time for the first day of enrollment, but sweetheart, your work is cut out."*

Me: *"I assure you that I will write both letters just as soon as we're done talking, and I want to thank you for all of the help you've given me today. I will contact you after I submit the letters to your superintendent."*

Mr. Burke: *"It was my pleasure Mrs. Christie. I look forward to that phone call. You have a good day. Good-bye."*

Me: *"Good-bye."*

Now at this point you've read several chapters of this book. So you already know how I responded to what just happened here. Yep, you're absolutely right. I hung up the telephone and ran through the house hollering and screaming. The children started screaming too, and running behind me playfully. I believe it was because I startled them. I must have run three victory laps before stopping! They were asking me, "What happened mom?" "Tell us what happened!" I yelled, "Victory!" I then began jumping up and down again while saying to God, "Thank you! Thank you! Thank you!" I was so ecstatic! Wow! What a huge surprise! In case you forgot, this same guy laughed in my face and blatantly told me that he would make sure that Daniel did not enroll in his county. So, can you imagine how I felt talking to him again, while remembering this? Not to mention how foolish it would have been to bring it to his attention. It was as if he forgot what he had previously said. Well I certainly wasn't going to remind him.

After the phone call ended, the action began! I immediately called my local school district and requested the address including what floor the office was on. Afterwards I called the Clay County school district and requested the same information. I sat at the computer for a few minutes and composed the letters. At about that time my husband came home. Perfect timing. He rejoiced at hearing my story, and we agreed that I would give him a two hour break before I would leave to take the first letter to our school district office. Yes, I hand delivered the letters. You didn't think that I would take a chance and mail them did you? Besides, I needed to speak face to face with an administrator to emphasize the importance of the time frame that I was working within. The administrator told me that she was not sure if the superintendent was permitting any out- of- county transfers. I told her that, " I needed to speak to him." She responded that, "He was not available." I then told her that, " I would not accept "No" for an answer. I am a homeowner who pays taxes for public schooling, and I know my rights." Gimme a break!

Exactly five days after I stood in the office of our local school district, I received their response permitting Daniel to transfer to Clay County. On that same afternoon, I drove to Clay County and delivered the letter to their superintendent's office. I also spoke with an administrator there and told her that I was following the instructions of Mr. Burke, and that before I left the building, I was going to call him to let him know that I just delivered the required letters to the superintendent's office. What could she say but, "Ok"?

At about five o'clock that afternoon, I received a call from Mr. Burke: "Mrs. Christie, we have everything we need for Daniel's enrollment. Welcome back to Clay County. I will call Tyndale Elementary and let them know that you will be coming in to register Daniel for kindergarten. They will provide further information including an orientation date and the name of his teacher. Again welcome to our district. Have a great school year."

Butterflies

Yippee! Yippee! It was the first day of kindergarten for Daniel. But by the butterflies that I had in my stomach, you would have thought that I was the new student. Yes, I was very excited for him, but beneath the excitement I was dealing with the fact that this was again a new school and a new teacher. And this time, he would have not just one teacher assistant, but three. We were able to meet his new teacher, Mrs. Zager, at the school's orientation a few days earlier, but had not met the assistants. I was well pleased with Mrs. Zager. Her love for children was evident. Especially those with special needs. She assured me that her assistants shared the same compassion, and referred to them as her "team," meaning that they had been working together for several years. So here we were. Daniel's first day of kindergarten.

I walked him to class and stayed until the second bell rang. Mrs. Zager then told the parents that the ringing of the second bell indicated the start of the school day. So I gave him a big hug and kiss, told him that "I loved him and to have a good day." As I exited his class, I turned around and went back to him and whispered in his ear, "I'll pick you up after school."

It was a bittersweet walk back to the car. I began to miss him the moment that the door clicked behind me. Wiping the tears from my eyes made me want to run back inside and stay with him all day on this first day of school so that I could be his personal assistant and show him his way around the school. Because although he was learning to read, he still did not have much language. He learned and recognized words, but was still unable to communicate them properly. And when he did speak it was not related to the real world, nor to what was currently happening around him. Also, compared to his former school, this was a very big school! There were nearly 1,500 students in this kindergarten through sixth grade center. Nevertheless, knowing that the best decision was to allow him to be alone with his class so that he could become more independent, I went home.

As the days and weeks passed, it was obvious that Daniel's kindergarten year was a continuation of the previous school year in every sense of the word. Mrs. Zager's class consisted of only six students. And because there were three assistants, each student received plenty of individual help from her every day. Even the frequency of his therapies increased. He was now being seen two to three times a week for speech and occupational therapy. This included a weekly interactive group session with his entire class. He also participated in adaptive physical education every day, where he was introduced to kickball, soccer, basketball, and swinging. Did I say swinging? Shhhh. I do not want Daniel to hear that word. He acquired such a love for swinging until it was the only playground activity that he desired. I remember telling Mrs. Zager, "I'll bet he could set a new record for the longest time a child stays on a swing." However, there would be one slight problem. Who would be willing to push him? Because Daniel had not learned how to swing by himself.

Just as the therapies increased at school, they also increased at Dr. Buckley's office. In addition to his current plan of treatment, Mild Hyperbaric Therapy was implemented. So we traveled to her office three days a week for a one hour session. Because of the importance of the therapy, I was willing for him to miss an hour or two of the school day. We either went before school, or I picked him up early. The forty-five minute drive to Dr. Buckley's office was my time to invoke conversation from Daniel, but most of the time he did not respond. So it was often time to relax and listen to some good music.

I will never forget our first mild hyperbaric therapy session. I was well prepared with the items that were suggested to make the session a smooth one: a crunchy snack, such as pretzels to prevent ear popping, bottled water or other drink, gum, books, and a video. We would be in the chamber for one hour each session.

Daniel responded to this first session precisely in the manner that the doctor forewarned. He was very excited to take off his shoes and grab the video. The idea of eating pretzels while watching a movie was thrilling to him. Everything was going well until it was time to get inside of the oblong, tent-like, six foot long chamber. He panicked and took off running! He ran from one side of the room to the next trying to prevent me from catching him. He managed to fight off everyone who tried to help me. Finally I was able to catch him and convince him that he didn't have to be afraid. I then got inside of the chamber first, and afterwards Dr. Buckley and the therapist helped him inside where he relaxed for the next hour. I spent the time trying to keep the oxygen mask on his face, and his hands from pulling the zipper that sealed us inside of the chamber. At the end of the visit he walked and pulled my hand and told everybody, "Good-bye!" I laughed as we walked out of the office.

We'd been informed of all of the wonderful benefits of mild hyperbaric therapy, yet to keep in mind that the effects vary from child to child. It could also take several visits before any changes could be seen. We were encouraged to just believe that it was working, and to keep coming.

But low and behold, as we pulled out of the parking lot of the doctor's office, something extraordinary happened. I heard a little voice ask, "Mommy who is Jesus?" "Did you just ask me a question?" I excitedly responded. He didn't answer me so I looked in my rearview mirror at him. He was staring out the window, yet seemed to be attentive to the fact that he was waiting for me to answer him. "Jesus is God's son, I replied. He is the Savior of the world, and He is our healer. He is also the one who is going to make you well again." "Oh, Okay," He responded.

Yes, I know that I could have given him a more age appropriate answer, but I was in a state of total amazement! I could hardly believe my ears! Did he really ask me a question? He really did ask me a question! This was huge and I knew it! It was a major victory in the unfair and unfamiliar battle that we were fighting! Therefore for him to ask me, "Who is Jesus?" gave me the opportunity to once again remind myself that autism was a battle too big for me, but it was not even a match for God! The drive home was with much anticipation of seeing my husband and two other children. I could hardly wait to see their face upon hearing Daniel's great news. I also knew that I had to call Dr. Buckley and share the news with her.

Within a few days after our huge celebration of day one, we returned for our second mild hyperbaric therapy visit. I was ready for a repeat performance from Daniel. Any minute he was going to try to run out of the room in fear of the odd looking chamber. But much to my surprise he didn't run this time. Neither was he reluctant to get inside of the chamber. Instead he quickly took off his shoes as if he was getting into a carnival bounce house, reached for a DVD, and the portable DVD player. As we all watched in amazement, Dr. Buckley responded, "It happens this way nearly every time, with every child." Once we were snuggled inside I took a nap while Daniel watched his movie. Each subsequent visit was a great time of rest and relaxation for the both of us.

Amidst the afternoon visits for hyperbaric therapy, Daniel's teacher informed me that an evaluation was being planned for him, facilitated by the school psychologist. It would include the speech therapist, occupational therapist, Mrs. Zager, the general education first grade teacher, and others. She then handed me a very thick envelope with paperwork enclosed confirming what she said.

On the day of the meeting, I walked inside very calm and confident. Attending prior school evaluations prevented intimidation of any sort. Each specialist shared their notes about Daniel's kindergarten year, as well as presented their recommendation for first grade. Mrs. Zager left the meeting early, but stayed long enough to speak of his progress, and how amazed she was at his behavior. Very mannerable, quick to grasp new ideas, follows directions well, and having never displayed a meltdown. She also mentioned that she believed his diet played a major role in his progress, and therefore asked me to explain the GF/CF diet to the team.

I took my time explaining the diet, and that as a result of it and the implementation of supplements and mild hyperbaric therapy Daniel was becoming more aware of, and in touch with the real world. His speech was obviously progressing, and he seemed more confident.

After I was done sharing the GF/CF diet, the speech and language therapist shared her notes from the kindergarten school year. Her recommendation was that, "We go ahead and consent to Daniel being taught sign language since many of 'these kids' never gain verbal language." I could hardly believe that she ignored what I shared, and had the audacity to label and stereotype my son! When she was done, she asked me, "Do you have any questions?" I told her no, but I have a statement! "No! I do not want Daniel to learn sign language. He will talk again and have excellent verbal language skills. He is to continue his three thirty-minute speech and language therapy sessions each week here at school, and nothing less!"

Of course you can imagine how uncomfortable the other team members must have felt at that heated moment, but I didn't care. This person was just another typical overbooked therapist with a, "Yeah, Yeah, Yeah. if you've seen one, you've seen them all attitude." It was as if they practiced being curt and lacked sympathy. Sure, I can imagine the number of children she had seen with similar symptoms, and little progression, but she was not hired to offer a prognosis, but instead a plan of treatment!

By the time I spoke with Mrs. Zager again, I sensed that she heard about my conversation with the speech therapist. So I broke the ice by saying, "All children deserve a fair chance, and should not be stereotyped nor short changed. I know that Daniel will overcome these symptoms. I've already seen enough to keep my faith alive. I also know that at this time, I am his voice. He's counting on me, and I won't let him down."

Daniel went on to finish kindergarten with much progress made. Summer school was offered as an option to assure that he retained the knowledge he learned during the school year. I declined enrolling him because I knew that he would learn even more over the summer as I worked with him at home, and as we traveled. Besides, I had my own private summer camp for my kids, and swimming lessons were among the top three activities.

Mrs. Zager proved to be an excellent teacher for Daniel, and it was my desire for him to remain in her class since she taught grades kindergarten through six. Therefore I submitted my request in writing. However, I was told that only the principal could authorize the classroom assignment. So, you've already guessed what I did. That's right. I called and scheduled an appointment to meet with the principal. The meeting went well, and I was granted my request for Mrs. Zager to be Daniel's first grade teacher.

Moving Forward

Often throughout our journey I could hardly wait for Daniel's next visit with Dr. Buckley. He was progressing tremendously, and I wanted her to see what I was seeing. For example, he walked into his classroom one morning and boldly greeted his teacher and her assistants. "Good morning Mrs. Zager!" "Good morning!" Afterwards, he took his lunchbox from me. What he did next absolutely made my day! With much hand coordination, he waved at me and said, "Good-bye, Mom. I love you! Have a good day!" We all laughed with joy, but I especially felt overjoyed to hear such heart-felt words coming from my son. He was beginning to mimic what he saw and heard me do. For these were the very same words that I said to him each morning before kissing him and walking out of his classroom. I also noticed that he began to talk about his classmates. Most of them had returned from the previous school year. And there was one in particular who Daniel apparently considered his best friend. Camon. Nearly every day he shared what he and Camon did at recess: "Me and Camon swing." "Me and Camon tag." He also told me of the times when Camon had a meltdown, or got into trouble: "Camon bad and crying," he'd say. Daniel did not know what a meltdown was, but his description of Camon's actions, and Mrs. Zager's response alluded to a meltdown.

Every day we were watching a transformation right before our eyes! We knew to not underestimate what Daniel would do or say. There was such a huge difference between the autism diagnosis, and his current status. So, with our sleeves rolled up, we were ready to take on the next level of challenges.

Daniel learned personal hygiene skills in kindergarten. He learned how to clean his face and hands both after eating lunch, and after playing at recess. He also learned to properly brush his teeth after eating snacks. However, he still had not mastered potty training. Although Mrs. Zager and I discussed his toilet needs during the initial orientation, it did not pose a problem in his kindergarten year. The most he'd ever do in his pull-up was urinate. However, Mrs. Zager made it clear that should he have a bowel movement he would be responsible for cleaning himself and changing his pull-up. Well, now that he was in first grade, and eating more, including a larger variety of foods, I now had much to be concerned about. I knew that he had not learned to clean up after having a bowel movement. In fact, he was still afraid to "let go." So, one day while he was at school I went to the store and purchased two potty training videos. I was so excited! I could hardly wait for the school day to end! Once we were home and settled, I gave him an after school snack. Twenty minutes later I put the potty in front of the TV, sat him on it, and turned on the first video. I then told him, "Sit here until Mommy says to get up. Ok?" "Ok." He answered. Ten minutes into the video I checked to see if he had used the potty. He hadn't, so I sat him back on the potty. After another twenty minutes passed, I checked him again. He still had not used the potty. I decided to sit on the floor next to him and watch the video. The video was simply boring, both of them. It was no wonder he would not "let go." I believe had the videos been relaxing and entertaining he would have forgotten about the potty, and it would have happened naturally. I finally decided that he'd had plenty of time to "go" if he really needed to. So I turned off the video, put a fresh pull-up on him, and put away the potty. No sooner than I did, he decided to "go"---- in the pull-up. Oh well, back to the drawing board.

Whenever I brought up this subject at Dr. Buckley's office, she always reminded me to, "Keep trying, be patient, and never give up." So that was the prescription we followed.

Daniel easily adjusted to first grade, and I believe it was partly due to him having the same teaching staff, classroom, and classmates. Consistency proved to be of vital importance in many ways. The curriculum was also very similar to kindergarten, with one major addition. Fieldtrips! Lots and lots of fieldtrips! They were provided the same opportunities as the general education classes. In fact, they went to the same venues. Some of the finest venues in the area! Including the movie theatre. I was absolutely speechless at the whole idea because these were children with various autism symptoms, including meltdowns. In addition, the fieldtrips required all of the teaching staff and some of the therapists from the autism wing of the school to be on hand. I was also on hand. I attended every field trip. I went to be with my son. Sure, it was wonderful that a great portion of the staff went, but I would not have been able to rest knowing that he was off campus, out in the real world with limited communication skills, and susceptible to all kinds of stares, ill treatment, and misunderstanding. His needs were just too great! Therefore, without being invited, I made it known to his teacher that I would accompany him on every fieldtrip. Needless to say she was quite surprised. It was also obvious that this was not the norm. I even sensed that I was unwelcome, but no one had the audacity to tell me. My kind, yet firm disposition during the conversation revealed that my decision was non-negotiable. However, as a result of me being there, it gave me the opportunity to see how others interacted with the students. And yes, there were plenty of meltdowns. One child even ran away from the crowd. Immediately several teachers ran after him. They called him a "sprinter." Thankfully, they were able to catch him and return him back to the group. Although I stayed with Daniel's class during the fieldtrips, I only held his hand if he reached for mine. I gave him his space, and he enjoyed the comfort of knowing that mommy was there.

One of Daniel's favorite fieldtrips was to a local ranch. Having observed him at the zoo, I knew that he was fond of animals. However, since we did not have a pet at home, at that time, I did not know how fond he really was. The students were given the opportunity to pet and feed the livestock. I laughed as I watched Daniel grab a handful of food for the goats, but quickly dropped it when they came to eat it. He'd back away quickly, and then walk back up to the fence once the goat turned its back, or went to someone else for food. The highlight of the day was the pony ride! Each student rode a pony. Not knowing whether or not he would be afraid to sit on the pony, I focused the camera, but kept my eyes on him in case I needed to make a mad dash to his rescue. It turned out that he loved it, and didn't want to get off. The day ended with a hay ride that stopped in the middle of the pasture to allow the children to feed hay to the cows. When I reminisce about the opportunities the students were afforded, it warms my heart to know that such love and care is given to them, and they are not treated differently because of their challenges.

As I mentioned earlier in this chapter, a remarkable change occurred in Daniel's diet. He began to desire more of a variety of foods. He became a lover of freshly sliced deli turkey rolls, fruit, and cookies. He also enjoyed bite-sized turkey meat balls. There were days when I would bake as many as one hundred bite-sized turkey meat balls on a cookie sheet. Afterwards I would put them into a large freezer bag and freeze them until needed. That suggestion was made by a nutritionist whom I met through Dr. Buckley's office. Having food readily made was advantageous. It made mealtime less stressful, allowing me to respond to his hunger in a timely manner. Preparing his lunch became easy. It alleviated the need to go to a fast-food restaurant for a quick meal. I must mention here that I never imagined spending so much time in the kitchen. There were some gluten –free meals that I trashed because even I would not have eaten them. I spent money on numerous foods that Daniel firmly rejected! One specific item was a package of breakfast sausages. There were six individual sausage links. They looked like Italian sausages, and I was excited to give it to him for breakfast. However, when I put his plate in front of him, he picked up the sausage, smelled it, and then put it down. It never touched his mouth. That incident taught me to ask questions about the food before I purchased it. Even a taste test was welcomed in hopes that it was going to prevent me from tossing all new items into the trash.

As the school year continued, I met other members of the teaching staff, as well as parents. Whenever I met a parent, especially of one of Daniel's classmates, I'd share my story and offer Dr. Buckley's telephone number. Much to my surprise, the idea of their child overcoming autism was not quickly embraced. Some parents responded as if it was just too much trouble to do anything else. As if it was easier to just accept their current state, and live with it. The saddest part of all was that none of the families had a pediatrician who believed in total recovery from autism. They were all told that their child would be in that condition for the rest of his or her life. Well, I certainly could identify with the emotional aspect of this issue, but I also remembered that it was my changing pediatricians that led to the right one. Nevertheless, at this point I decided to just be cordial, and not pushy. I believed that at some point they would believe me. Hopefully before the school year ended.

As an advocate wanting to spread the word that autism was treatable, I quickly learned that it was important for me to realize that this news was clearly unheard of. In most areas it was considered as an incurable childhood disease. A renown doctor in our city had many autistic patients, and told the parents that there was no cure. Even most of the autistic students at Tyndale Elementary were patients of his. So, it was no wonder that my conversation was not received. And although I had a child who was recovering, I was not the authority on this subject. I was not the doctor.

My resolve then was to give it time, and allow them to see Daniel's growth for themselves. They were not familiar enough with his past to know just how great his progress was. However, our closest relatives and friends could certainly see the difference. Ms. Lucille, a dear friend and personal childcare minister for our family knew Daniel from his infancy. For years she traveled with us when I was in music full-time, as well as when my husband and I needed to travel alone. She kept the kids for us at our home. As a result of Daniel's progress, it made her job easier, especially when out in the public. There was no longer anxiety about him running up on the stage, or of him trying to wander off. He would sit mannerly just like his brother and sister.

My parents also witnessed his progress. Daddy would often say to me, "He's calmer." Whereas Momma took note of the fact that he was eating a more balanced diet.

We soon branched out and began to visit out of town relatives, and stay in their home during our visit. It really allowed us to enlighten them about Daniel's condition. What always amazed them was that they had to take our word for it, because, with the exception of potty training, there was no evidence of what he had been through. They would watch him enjoying playing with the other children, as the children also enjoyed him. If they got into some mischief, they were all scolded, even Daniel. One such scenario was regarding a pretty steep staircase that led to the second floor of the house. Can you imagine how much fun the children had running up and down those stairs, and jumping from the third step to the floor, over and again? Well, when their aunt finally scolded them, their faces looked as if she scared the living daylights out of them! Daniel wasn't used to it, but he quickly stopped jumping, and left the room with the other children. We had a good laugh after they cleared the room.

Family outings became more frequent. They included the movies, shopping malls, restaurants, parks, supermarkets, car dealerships, music concerts, family reunions, theme parks, resorts, birthday parties, and our favorite place---the beach.

My children have always loved our trips to the beach. However, during his toddler years, Daniel was terrified of the water. He would run from it as if it was chasing him. When we encouraged him to just put his foot into it he would scream and fight to get away. On one occasion, although he was crying, my husband picked him up and walked out into the water, promising to not put him in it. He trusted his dad at that time, but he never consented to it again.

For three consecutive summers we attended swimming lessons at the neighborhood swim club, but to no avail. It was like pulling tongue and teeth to get Daniel to step down into the pool. During his lesson he fought the instructor and cried the entire time. He made so much noise until I just finally told her that we would give it more time for him to like the water. Once he saw his brother and sister in the water with the instructor, he would step onto the first step while holding on to the rail. But if we looked in his direction, he would hurriedly get out of the pool. I cannot tell you how aggravated I was! It was so important to me for him to learn how to swim.

At some point during his recovery from autism, he acquired a love for the water. Today, both our beach and swimming pool outings are full of fun and laughter. He enjoys basking in deep water with his dad and brother at his side. It's a totally new attitude towards water! Although he has yet to learn to swim, I'm sure that his next swimming lesson will be successful!

No, Not Even a Chicken Wing!

One of Daniel's favorite foods is buffalo wings, especially my GF/CF (Gluten-free/Casein-free), crispy, garlic, oven-fried recipe. He's learned how to eat the meat and then enjoy the bones. It's enough to make a dog mad! I can't name too many things that he's willing to sacrifice a chicken wing for, but on this one occasion, the chicken met it's match against a potato sack race!

On a beautiful Saturday morning in April 2007, we attended Family Fun Day at Faith Christian Center, the church we attend. The grounds were filled with excitement as families drove onto the parking lot, ready to experience a full day of carnival-style fun, food, entertainment, and fellowship! The children ran across the grass as they were drawn to colorful inflatable bounce houses. They could either jump and tumble in one, or rock-climb and slide down the others. For those who wanted to show their competitive side, there were games of basketball and volleyball. The smell of barbeque filled the air as chefs and chef-wanna-be's showed off their "ancient family secret" recipes.

We strolled across the campus to greet family and friends. Some were sitting in lounge chairs. Some were relaxing on large picnic blankets, and others just stood around enjoying conversation.

The chatter from the basketball court attracted my then five-foot ten, eleven year old son. He made his way over to the court and spent most of his time there. The idea of him jumping inside one of the bounce houses may have caused us to be ejected from the carnival!

My husband and I found ourselves in line for two different attractions. One for my daughter, and the other for Daniel. Daniel decided earlier that he wanted to hang out with daddy, so my daughter and I enjoyed the "mommy-daughter" time together.

I followed her from attraction to attraction, while keeping an eye on my elder son, and playfully waving at my husband and Daniel from across the way. I smiled as Daniel completed one attraction and ran to another. I watched my husband trotting trying to keep up. Then finally I saw them standing still. They were sharing a plate of buffalo chicken wings, while standing on the sidelines and observing the potato sack race.

The potato sack race was another one of the carnival's "hot spots." The crowd of observers there was larger than the one at the basketball court. The children participating in the race were older, taller, and seemed to be very skillful at it. My husband felt the same about them. However, without warning Daniel ran over to the race, picked up a potato sack, and got in line. My husband looked at the children that he would be racing, and decided that this might not be a good idea for Daniel. He didn't want him to be embarrassed. So he called his name and showed him the plate of buffalo chicken wings. Daniel immediately ran over to get one, but kept looking back at the race. My husband tried to engage in conversation with him, while making sure that he kept eating the wings. Daniel continued to look back at the race, as if he was checking to see if it was almost his turn. He really wanted to be in the race, but my husband didn't agree, so he tried to hold him. Evidently Daniel caught on to the "chicken wing plot" because he quickly ate it, put the bone on the plate, wiggled himself free from my husband's hand, and ran back over to the race. He ran too quickly for Daddy to stop him. Had he tried, the plate of "wings" might have ended up in the sand.

My husband then understood how important the race was to Daniel. He saw that his heart was in it. Determination! So he stood back and watched from the sidelines.

Daniel handled the potato sack like a pro! Stepping into it one foot at a time. The facilitator walked onto the field, took her place and began the race. "On your mark!" Daniel looked straight ahead waiting for the next command. "Get Set!" He put his "game face" on and leaned forward! "Go!"

Like a leaping antelope, Daniel galloped down the field. With sheer amazement on his face my husband laughed as he watched him standing tall, and keeping his balance! As he moved towards the halfway mark, he kept a steady jumping rhythm. Never looking to the left nor the right. He was focused on finishing the race. As he approached the finish line, there were screams of encouragement for each of the participants from supportive onlookers. My husband was jumping and yelling, "Go Daniel! Go Daniel!" Daniel undoubtedly heard him because that's exactly what he did. He kept going and going! Ignoring all of the distractions! Even the yelling of his name.

The roaring cheers from the observers provoked many others to come over to witness the race. It was a heated race! Even those who fell got up and continued the race, so everyone that entered was headed toward the finish line. The crowd was totally ballistic! Then suddenly the whistle blew! "We have a winner!" "Daniel Christie!"

What? He did it! He really did it! He won the potato sack race! He was confident that this was something he knew how to do, and he proved it to us! My husband ran over to him laughing, yet dumbfounded. He picked him up and continued to cheer him on, "Daniel, you won the race!" "Yes I know. Daddy where's my prize?" was the response that came from our little winner. Everyone that heard him laughed. Then he and daddy went over to the facilitator and claimed his prize. He ran to me and said, "Look Mommy, I won the race and got a prize!" I was absolutely speechless! I was so proud of him! All I could do was laugh. I was tickled with joy!

Oh the thrill of knowing that my little boy accomplished something so big! Even he was proud of himself! I was greatly moved by this, because it was not a "special Olympics" event for children with autism, or special needs. But it was a race with normal, healthy children. Some were even older than him.

We celebrated for days! We called our parents, siblings, friends, etc. and told them about it. That day Daniel made us take the limits off of him. He showed us that not only is he an overcomer, but also a winner! We saw that he was beginning to make up for lost time. Therefore we had to "get out of the way" and allow him new and wonderful experiences. The emotions that brought fear and negative "what if" questions had to be annihilated. Our little boy was back, and ready to live! Ready to enjoy his childhood!

It was amazing to learn just how much he'd overcome. There was a time when he didn't understand most of what he was exposed to in our everyday living. But the days and months following the potato sack race unveiled a new mind. It began with him starting to ask questions. His question could be about anything, and I do mean anything. For example if we were going to the mall, he'd ask, "Where are we going?" My response would be, "To the mall." Then he'd ask, "What's a mall?" and so on. Nearly every conversation in his presence prompted questions. If he was not satisfied with the answer, he would ask more questions. Usually, why or why not. Even when he watched a movie by himself, he'd pause it and come and ask me the meaning of something in the movie. After he would walk away, I'd look up to the ceiling, wink my eye, and tell the Lord, "Thank You!" I still do it today.

Each year my older children submit both their birthday and Christmas wish list in writing. For the past two years, Daniel's has been included. He will request to shop at a specific store to purchase his gift, because he gets his ideas from the Saturday morning commercials during the time he's watching cartoons. Whatever the hottest toy or video game advertised, he is sold! Not only sold, but also convinced that the toy store mentioned in the commercial is the one where we must buy his gifts, especially since he may be greeted by a giraffe. Don't worry moms and dads. The giraffe is not alive. But they are all over the toy store! Some of you know which toy store I'm referring to. I see you smiling and nodding your head.

Speaking of video games, Daniel is quite a whiz when it comes to electronics. He operates a computer very well. So well that we had to set up a separate work station for him at home, so that our main computer would be available to us without delay. He has learned to surf the net. It is common to hear him laughing because he's looking at a cartoon or one of his favorite movies. One day before he signed off, he came and asked me, "Mommy do you want to check your e-mail?" I laughed and said to him, "What do you know about e-mail?" He just smiled at me.

Each year prior to Spring Break we'd ask our children for vacation ideas. Because we live in Florida, the beach is always an option. And so are the theme parks in Central Florida. For the last two years Daniel has chosen our Spring Break theme park. Of course with the agreement of his siblings. Daily we'd watch him sign on the computer and surf the different theme parks. He'd even take a virtual tour, becoming familiar with every ride and attraction. Then over the next several months leading up to vacation time, he'd suggest the park over and again. Even call us over to the computer to view it with him. Last year he chose Disney's Animal Kingdom. It was the perfect park! He was absolutely delighted as he saw a conglomerate of animals! He was our tour guide, making sure that we didn't miss anything. His favorite spot was the "Festival of the Lion King." It was a production that left us in awe. We spent the entire day at the park. It turned out to be another wonderful family vacation!

Since then we've been to other theme parks, and have also added cruises to our vacation options. We're currently making plans for another vacation. However we choose to spend it, I guarantee you that the fun will be endless, the moments will be special, and the memories will last for more than a lifetime.

One day I'll share these stories with my grandchildren, of how no one can stop the determination in the heart of a winner. And that even the greatest challenges can be overcome if we are willing to let nothing deny us. Nothing! No, not even a chicken wing! And then we'll laugh!

Pineapple Poop!

Have you ever awakened to a new day and sensed that it would be very special or extraordinary? I mean you wake up with an "I can't explain it, but I just sense that something good is going to happen to me today" feeling all over you. Well, let me tell you what followed this great "feeling" on this particular day!

It was December 4, 2007. My oldest son's birthday! Which meant celebration time and personal royal treatment for him all day long. He was relieved from all chores and household duties, and was to be catered to throughout the day, including me taking to him the lunch of his choice, along with cupcakes to include his classmates in the celebration.

So on that exciting morning, I woke up and made a nice breakfast for the family. Afterwards I went to my oldest son's room and whispered in his ear, "Happy Birthday, Sweetheart." With his eyes still closed, he mustered up a weak, yet sincere smile. Shortly afterwards he got out of the bed. I then went to Daniel's bed and whispered, "Good Morning, Poogee." Within a few minutes he too was out of the bed.

At this point I thank God for my paying attention to Daniel when he walked past me, because what I saw was nothing short of a miniature carpet disaster! As he walked past me he made a swishing sound with every step. Now I knew what a soiled pull-up looked like, but never had I heard one make a swishy sound. So immediately I ran to stop him in his path, felt the pull-up, and discovered what was swishing. He had a terrible case of diarrhea! The pull-up that he was wearing had become soiled, big, bulgy and thick. Another step on foot could have been the difference between clean sweet smelling carpet versus soiled odor-filled carpet. Picking him up, I ran to my bedroom, threw back the covers on my bed, put him on it, and got to work: Removed the pull-up, applied baby wipes, and more baby wipes. I rubbed on the lotion, put Daniel on a new pull-up, and fresh clothes. Within seconds of me dressing him again, he got up and went into the family room. I was nearly exhausted! Remember, by this time Daniel was eight years old. I not only picked him up, but also ran while holding him. I just couldn't take a chance on anything dripping from the pull-up!

The incident caused me to fall behind in my morning routine. In addition to making sure that my daughter was up, I still needed to iron clothes, make lunches, and get everyone to school on time. Due to the fact that Daniel had diarrhea, he would not be attending school. Keeping him at home was not only the right thing to do, but also complying with the school's guidelines. I called my husband at work and told him about all of the morning's challenges. He laughed! Followed by words of encouragement, and a suggestion to take my time driving in the early morning traffic.

Finally, after everyone was fed and dressed, we headed out the door. As we listened to the radio, I called in to the request line and dedicated a song to my oldest son in honor of his birthday. It was a nice way to restart the day. It made him smile.

Daniel and I returned home after taking my other children to school. I called Mrs. Zager to let her know that he would not be there possibly for the next two days. She certainly understood. I now had to figure out why Daniel had diarrhea. There were no signs or symptoms of illness. He had not complained of his tummy hurting. And he still seemed pretty content.

I just happened to be in the same room with Daniel when I heard the fast squirting sound again. I quickly grabbed him by the hand and ran into the bathroom. I figured if something was going to come out, it would fall onto the linoleum which would be a much easier job to clean up. So we stood there listening for the finish. Afterwards I changed his pull-up and put on a fresh one. Within the first hour of returning home, he soiled four pull-ups. I became concerned and called his pediatrician. This was anything but normal.

After speaking to the pediatrician and answering her initial questions, I was taken by surprise at one particular question, "What does it look like?" I then realized that I had not taken the time to look at it. I responded, "I don't know. I didn't really look at it. It seemed all watery to me." She suggested that I look at it and call her back. So, while I waited for Daniel to soil another pull-up, I realized that if he continued at the pace he was going, he was going to use all of his pull-ups. Therefore, I needed to somehow encourage him to use the toilet, instead.

I tried to stay near him. It was pretty easy since he was watching TV in the family room, and I was in the kitchen, which is connected to the family room. I attempted to make myself some breakfast, but was distracted by more squirting. Once again I grabbed Daniel's hand and ran into the bathroom. I quickly pulled down his pull-up and sat him on the toilet seat. He sat there with his head resting on both palms like a thinker. I ran and got him some books from his book collection. He sat there reading, and was content to see me sitting on the floor. I told him that, "I wanted him to "go" in the toilet and not in his pull-up." The look in his eyes was that of fear. I assured him that "There was nothing to be afraid of, and that I would be right there with him." I asked him if he would like for me to give him a special treat, such as a new book, as well as do my victory dance for him? He nodded his head and smiled. "Okay then, go ahead and let go in the toilet." It took a few seconds. And then the squirting began. "Yes, that's it Daniel!" "Mommy's big boy!" "Good job!" I said. Followed by me clapping and dancing all over the bathroom!

Upon finishing in the bathroom, I prepared to put another pull-up on him, but remembered that I had not looked at his soiled pull-up. So, I picked it up and looked at it.

"Pineapples." "Pineapples?" When did he eat pineapples? "Oh, at breakfast two days ago." No, actually for the past two days he's eaten pineapples for breakfast! "Two days in a row?" I forgot that pineapples were rough on his system! It's no wonder he has diarrhea! "Oh Daniel, please forgive me. I wasn't thinking clearly."

After putting a pair of underpants on him, I called the pediatrician back. My explanation was very short. She told me that it was good news! Her remedy was simple. "Keep him hydrated with clear liquids."

Relieved to know the cause of his diarrhea, I now had to focus on helping him to use the toilet every time he needed to "go," because it was certain that I would run out of pull-ups if I didn't. So, I told him, "Sweetheart, if you feel that you're about to 'go' in your underwear, run to the bathroom and sit on the toilet. Mommy will be with you to dance and celebrate! Ok?" He responded, "Ok."

We returned to the kitchen and family room. While he watched his favorite shows, breakfast was back in the works. Upon finishing breakfast I went into the children's bedroom and began some house cleaning. As I walked through the living room towards my bathroom with a handful of dirty clothes, without warning Daniel ran past me at high speed towards my bathroom, too. Immediately realizing what was going on I dropped the clothes and ran behind him. He was running and trying to pull down his underpants at the same time. Moving quickly to help him, he made it just in time! And my celebration of clapping and dancing instantly began. Followed by more acclamations. Although he didn't say it, it was easy to see that he was proud of himself! This whole ordeal lasted from breakfast time to noon. By 12 o'clock Daniel was completely potty trained! He had even learned how to clean himself after using the toilet!

I was trying to process all that had happened that morning. It left me exhausted and speechless, yet full of joy! Daniel mastered potty training! He really did it! He was finally, completely potty trained! And it was as a result of eating pineapples! Can you believe that! Now don't you know had I known that pineapples would be the key to him mastering potty training, my pantry shelves would have been stacked with cans of pineapples, and possibly a fresh one in the refrigerator.

I settled down enough to call my husband at work and my mom to share the good news. They both laughed, and thought that it was a very humorous story.

Now to me, this was the highlight of the year 2007! And it just so happened that it occurred in December. However, there were other major milestones earlier in the year. For example, he learned to swing without needing someone to push him. I absolutely loved to push him when at the park. We'd make up silly counting games. He even enjoyed other children swinging next to him, but he didn't like for me to push them. He'd fuss and make it known that I belonged to him. Sometimes it was a bit embarrassing, especially when the parents of these children would end their bench conversations to come to help their child. Therefore, on Valentine's Day 2007, it was the best gift of the day when Mrs. Zager met me at the car rider's area to excitedly tell me, "Daniel learned to push himself on the swing, today! He no longer need us to push him!"

Another milestone was his academic progress. He began to exceed the goals and benchmarks in his Individual Education Plan (IEP). He was reading above grade level, as well as greatly improving in his language skills. Amongst all of the academic success, I especially took note of his ability to memorize well. He not only displayed an exceptional memory, but also asked questions that were relevant to our conversations.

His teacher took note of his tremendous success. She often made comments such as, "Daniel's doing well!" I especially liked to hear her say, "Boy was he talking up a storm today!"

On one particular afternoon, she came to me and said that, "The other teachers have been asking me about Daniel's progress, and would like to know more about his diet, and the other components of his progress." At the end of our conversation, she asked me if I would talk to the teachers and staff of the autism area. I agreed, and set a date to come in on an afternoon, at the end of the school day.

On the evening before the meeting, I looked into the pantry and cabinets to see if there were any new, unopened boxes of the products that Daniel ate. I was pleasantly surprised to find several, so I bagged them and set them aside to take with me on the next day. The day of our special meeting finally arrived. I made sure that I was at the school in plenty of time to both pick up Daniel, and to set up for the presentation. Not only did I have food for them to sample, but I also had empty containers, such as his almond milk carton, to allow them to see what other products I buy for him, and for them to view the nutritional value information on each product.

Before the teachers and staff arrived, I stood back and took a final glance at my set-up. I was impressed! It looked professionally done! Soon afterwards everyone arrived, and the presentation began. I simply shared with them my story about Daniel's initial symptoms, the office visit with Dr. Buckley, and the fact that he was now in the recovery stage. Gaining ground every day.

Although most of them were well informed of autism symptoms, I still chose to highlight a few facts about it:

Autism Facts

1) One in every 90 children born in the U.S. has autism

2) Autism strikes boys more often than girls – roughly one in 80 boys are affected with autism.

3) Autism is the fastest growing developmental disability in the U.S. today.

4) Autism is more prevalent among children than diabetes, cancer and pediatric AIDS combined.

5) The lifelong costs associated with an autistic individual is estimated between 3 and 5 million dollars

Signs of Autism

Nonexistent or poor eye contact.

Lack of imaginative play or imitation.

Prefers to be alone-may have social skills deficits, may respond negatively to crowds.

Reactions to pain that appear aggressive or self-injurious.

May experience difficulty speaking or expressing needs-they may use pointing, gestures versus words, and often have tantrums.

Recurring lengthy or chronic infections.

At the end of the presentation I answered questions from the staff. I was amazed at how much knowledge I'd gained over the years. After all of the questions were answered, I invited everyone to sample the products that were on display. They included some of his GF/CF snack foods: crackers, cookies, and chips. The other packaged items on the table included GF/CF spaghetti, brown rice, almond milk, vegan cheese, waffles, sausages, ketchup, garlic powder, onion powder, frozen ground turkey, applesauce, and bread. The staff was very surprised at the variety of foods available for such a special diet, and how tasty most of them were. The meeting concluded with Dr. Buckley's contact information being made available.

We're Ready!

Well Daniel was certainly turning heads! He was not only the hot topic among the staff, but also among the parents. Those same parents who I tried to reach out to several months earlier were now ready to hear about the steps we were taking towards Daniel's recovery. For the past two years when we arrived in the afternoon to pick up our child, we did not have much to talk about. If we arrived too early, most of us took a nap. However, all of that changed. The naptime became a Q & A session. As I talked to parents one on one, it was amazing to me that each of them pretty much asked the same questions. Then there were the kind comments: "Wow! Daniel is doing great!" "He's talking more and seems very alert!" "What exactly are you doing for him?" Then there were the very assertive parents: "Just tell me what you're doing for Daniel!" "What's going on with Daniel? He's really changed." And finally, the overbearing, anxious parent: "Mrs. Christie, just give me the doctor's information and I'll call her myself!"

Now although some parents approached me in a somewhat distasteful manner, I overlooked their behavior, and extended my compassion. They were finally convinced that their child could overcome this ugly condition, and live a happy, fulfilling life, beginning in their childhood. So, for some parents it seemed the hardest request in the world to ask me for the information because they had ignored it for a very long time. I didn't care about that, and I tried to make sure that they knew that I didn't. I was on their side! I was so excited for these parents, and even more so, for their child. A key to a child overcoming autism is parental involvement. Every child needs an advocate! The advocate is the voice or person speaking on behalf of the child. The advocate also has the awesome responsibility of making sure that the child receives all of the medical services needed to become whole and healed again. Which means you take them to their doctors' visits, therapy sessions, and everywhere else they must go as a part of the healing process. It also includes you doing your own research, staying aware of current news, and especially asking questions.

The role of an advocate can often be a tiring one, but the motivation to continue comes from knowing that your child is counting on you to help them. So you can understand why the idea of these parents being ready brought me so much joy!

My instructions to them were very simple: First, contact Dr. Buckley and make an appointment for her to see your child. Next, remove all wheat gluten and casein (dairy) products from your child's diet, and replace them with gluten-free and casein free products.

Now before any of them could panic, I immediately interjected that, "I would not only volunteer to go grocery shopping with them, but also come over and cook a few meals and snacks. Most of all I made them a promise to be there for them as they began their child's journey to recovery.

The first family's shopping trip included two grocery stores: A health food store, and one that was part of a popular grocery store chain. We spent nearly an hour in both, walking up and down each aisle. Using a comparison chart, we discussed how to read the ingredients, and recognize the different names of wheat gluten and casein that is found in most foods, including malt vinegar. How surprised they were to see some of the same foods in both stores. However, the regular grocery store offered it at a much lower price. Which presented the wonderful topic of comparison shopping. As aforementioned in a previous chapter, there were times when food was tossed into the trash after being cooked, and refused by Daniel. My first experience shopping at the health food store was quite costly. It was a solo trip. The only guidance was from one of the employees who simply said, "There are labels on the shelves for each product. Orange is for gluten free, yellow for casein free, and green for peanut free." After her instructions I walked up and down every aisle, reading nearly every food item of my interest. Three hours and too much money later, the first order of GF/CF grocery went home with me. The high cost of food is what sparked my interest in inquiring about the same products in regular grocery stores. And would you know that most of the products on my list were found on their shelves. However, there were some foods that I still had to purchase, and even preferred to purchase from the health food store. The health food store also served as a great reference for new products on the market. They usually received them first. Comparison shopping allowed me to equally appreciate both.

Just to mention another family, it was a great idea for me to visit their home. The mom seemed to be doing well with purchasing the GF/CF foods. However, she kept speaking negatively about it, and her son seemed to respond accordingly. Choosing to be pessimistic, she lacked the desire to do what was best for him. And in the little that she did, she complained. She'd often say, "There's no way that he's going to eat this. He's used to eating regular foods. I can't fool him." On one occasion when she completely wanted to give up, she expressed it to me by saying, "I don't think that this is going to work." Empathetically I said to her, "I understand how you feel, but I can't let you give up." So we made a pact. She was required to keep all of her appointments with Dr. Buckley, follow the GF/CF diet, and give it time to work. If it didn't work within a reasonable amount of time, I would refund her for all of her GF/CF grocery purchases. Now the pact seemed a bit much especially on my part since no one knows how a child's progress will be from day to day. Nevertheless, we laughed about it, and she was encouraged to keep trying. About a month later she met me in the parking lot after school to tell me that her son's language was clearer, he was now much calmer at home, and sleeping through the night. I jokingly told her that, "I didn't believe her, because she said that none of this was not going to work for her."

There are other stories that could be mentioned; however this next family's story cannot be omitted. On one particular evening I received a phone call from a family in South Florida. Both parents were on the phone. They informed me that another family referred them to me because of my son's recovery from autism. They had heard of Dr. Buckley, and would soon be in the area to keep their son's appointment with her. Their knowledge of the DAN! process was little to none. Nevertheless, they were encouraged by their friends' testimony about Daniel, and was provoked to get him the help that he needed. During the conversation I was asked many questions about my son's pre and post autism demeanor. Trying to answer all of the questions to their satisfaction, more questions arose as a result of some of the comments that I made. The phone call was very lengthy. At the end of the conversation, the mother asked me if they could see Daniel while they were visiting the area. Knowing that this would give them a greater sense of hope, I consented to it.

On the evening that they arrived, I received a phone call from them stating that they were at a restaurant in my neighborhood. It was pretty late, but because I had given them my word, I met them there. Daniel was already in bed for the evening, so he did not accompany me. Upon entering the restaurant, I saw the family sitting in an area near the back. Much to my surprise, there were nearly twenty persons present. As we greeted, they motioned for me to order some food, as they would pay for it. Graciously refusing to order, I welcomed them to the city and began to share Daniel's story in detail. As the evening was coming to a close, the mother asked me if we could meet on the next day so that they could see Daniel. After choosing a park, we agreed upon what time we would meet.

The next day my kids and I arrived at the park several minutes before the other family. It allowed me time to walk around the park and to make sure that there were no surprise openings, nor unlocked entrances besides the main entrance. My kids all chased one another, and Daniel eventually went to the swing. Once the other family arrived, we were well engaged in playing. I called my kids over and introduced them. As the older two ran to resume playing, I detained Daniel for a moment and allowed the parents to take a closer look at him, and to listen to him converse with me. Finally, he decided that it was time to play again, and ran over to the slide. Suddenly without warning, angrily, the mother stood up and said, "I don't believe that he had autism!" "He doesn't act like a child with autism!" Shocked at her behavior, I responded, "He did have autism!" "We have lived the past five years of our lives dealing with the most challenging situation that we've ever faced as a family, and you think that we made this up? Do you know how much pain my heart has felt, or how much I've cried, and wondered what was this that we were dealing with, and why my child? Do you have any idea of how it felt not having an answer for the first two years, and once the answer did come, to learn that it was the most controversial childhood disease on the planet? Have you any idea of how long I've prayed and believed God for this moment when Daniel would come to the playground and play with not just other children, but his own brother and sister? Well, you're looking at an answer to my prayers! He's been through a lot, but God is manifesting healing in his body, and we're enjoying every minute of it!" I brought him here to give you hope. It hasn't been so long a time ago when I was where you are now. I didn't have another family to encourage me in this manner. Had it not been for Dr. Buckley, and the few parents looking for answers who I met with every Tuesday night, I might have felt alone. But since they were there for me, I feel the obligation to reach out to other families who are in this storm, to give them hope of what faith in God will do!"

She apologized and said that, "Daniel looks and acts like a normal boy his age, and it was hard to imagine him having autism." I told her that that's a compliment to God! We remained at the park for another half hour. It was a time of more encouragement for them to continue believing that God can and will heal their son, and to do their part of continuing his office visits and following Dr. Buckley's instructions.

After they returned to South Florida we continued to talk often. The years have now passed on, and we don't talk anymore, but it's a great feeling knowing that our paths crossed. I look forward to seeing them again!

As we counted the parents who inquired about the DAN! process, there were nearly ten families who became new patients of Dr. Buckley. Not to mention the many families that we met while out shopping, at restaurants, church, at the park, or just in passing. If our paths crossed a family who had an autistic child, I took the time to introduce us, tell a quick summary of Daniel's story, refer them to Dr. Buckley, as well as recommend Tyndale Elementary School.

All of the excitement felt like we were a part of a new revolution! The thrill of it all somehow overshadowed the fact that the end of the school year had come. Third grade seemed to sneak upon us like a friend hiding in a bush! So much had been accomplished, especially during the second half of the school year! As we once again prepared to say good-bye to the teachers and students, such a sense of family was felt. Tears flowed at the same time that hugs and smiles were exchanged. Mrs. Zager cried more than everyone else, and before we could comfort her, she lovingly said, " Oh, I do it every year. If I didn't I'd think that something was wrong with me." Before leaving the classroom, I told her that I will again request that Daniel be placed in her class for his third grade year, especially since it was a great fit.

A New Direction

Sum, sum, summertime was here again and the glorious school break that every student looks forward to! An excitement filled our home as we listened to the constant talking of our once silent chatterbox. His laughter and playfulness allowed no place for gloom and despair. With a desire to run and play tag in the house, we took it as a hint to seek out some parks with plenty of room to roam. So while we drove around looking for parks in our area, I realized that there needed to be a balance of fun, continual learning, and hyperbaric therapy visits. The easiest way to convince him that we would still have fun, along with going to therapy, was to make up a schedule. Therefore I suggested to each of my kids to give me a list of what they would like to do, and we would then sit down, look over the lists, and make a master schedule. Well, it didn't take long for them to make their list, and much to my surprise they chose some of the same ideas. After we made the master schedule, we felt that it was the official sign of the summer break! And off we went into it!

On one particular day my daughter brought to me some restaurant coupons that she received along with her report card. The coupons were for the students to receive a special treat, free of charge, as a result of them making the honor roll, having outstanding conduct, and excellent attendance. She asked me if we could go to the restaurants throughout the summer so that she could redeem her coupons. Of course my answer was, "Yes!" Evidently my oldest son heard her talking to me, because shortly afterwards he presented his coupons also. At that moment I realized that I had not looked at their final report card. So I told them to bring me their report card. While reading them, it was such an awesome feeling to see how well they did! They were certainly deserving of the rewards they received, and I was so proud of them!

The first three weeks of summer went by without one moment of boredom. Amidst the kids' schedule of fun, I still found quiet time for me. It was usually after their eight-thirty bedtime. It was nice watching a movie and eating popcorn in the stillness of the evening. During one of my quiet times, it dawned on me that I forgot to look at Daniel's final report card. So right then and there I quietly went into his bedroom and picked up his book bag. I returned to the sofa and pulled out his report card. His grades were excellent! He was shining! And then I turned over the report card to see the place where the teacher indicates whether a student was promoted or retained, and to my shocking surprise, Mrs. Zager had written in the word, "retained!" "What!" "Retained?" "This has to be a mistake!" The next few hours were spent trying to figure out how she came to this conclusion considering that it was a stellar year for him both academically and socially. Anger was setting in. Somehow I fell off to sleep. It was the best thing for me to do!

Daybreak came and brought on my brand new agenda! I needed to know who was to blame for such a huge error! It was time for some answers! My first phone call was to the main office at Tyndale Elementary. Since Mrs. Zager taught summer school each year, I just knew that she would be in her classroom, and available to talk. But when the office told me that she was not teaching summer school, it only made me more anxious for an answer. So I asked to speak to the assistant principal. Without hesitation I was transferred to her, and she patiently listened to my entire story. Once I was done, she simply responded by saying, "I'm as surprised as you are. However, only Mrs. Zager can explain or change this. And she is not scheduled to be back until early August." I understood her response, but it was not good enough. I thanked her, and told her that I will try to reach Mrs. Zager at the phone number that she gave to the parents. As I hung up the phone, there was a sense of peace knowing that this was an error, and that it could be corrected. It was just a matter of finding the phone number and locating Mrs. Zager.

Shortly afterwards, I found the phone number along with other contact information for her class. Immediately calling the number, I was able to locate her. When she answered the phone, I greeted her and said that I called to discuss Daniel's report card. I also told her that I called the school and was surprised to know that she was not teaching summer school. She then responded that she decided to spend her summer vacationing with family in another part of the country. As the conversation continued, I went on to say that, "The reason I called was because Daniel's report card indicate that he has been retained in the second grade, and I know that this is an error. Especially considering the outstanding year he had both academically and socially. I need to know if you are aware of this, and if so, why, and how are you going to correct this?" Now let me mention here that I was not irate. I highly respected Mrs. Zager, and I knew that the feeling was mutual. However, her response to my questions was very dumbfounding! She stated, "Mrs. Christie you are correct. Daniel did well this school year. As a matter of fact he did very well and that is the problem. I've never had a student to complete the second grade curriculum, at the first attempt, as well as he did. And according to what he accomplished, he should be placed into a self-contained, third grade class next school year, but I wasn't sure if he was ready. Since I wasn't sure, I decided to keep him in the autism area for another year." "But that's not fair to Daniel!" I responded. "We expect him to do well! We expect him to overcome all of the symptoms and challenges that he has, which is why we put him on the GF/CF diet, the supplements, and the therapies. They are not to be a part of him for the remainder of his life. We look for positive change to let us know that he is continually moving forward, and this is one of those signs that lets us know that he is. Now you are his teacher, but this decision should have been discussed with my husband and I. The final decision is ours. And because Daniel is proving that he can do the work, he deserves every chance to excel. Therefore, I'm asking you to please correct his report card to indicate that he is promoted to the third grade, and we will make sure that he is in the correct class next school year, and receive the help he need both at school, and at home." She apologized and said that she was not scheduled to return home until later in the summer. However, after our call ends, she would contact the assistant principal to inform her about the decision made as a result of our conversation. And once she was home, she would make the correction in writing and update his file. She also told me that she would contact me once it was done. I told her to enjoy her summer vacation, and that I looked forward to talking to her soon.

While still in a state of disbelief, my next phone call was to my husband to share this information with him. Once we were done talking, it was time for me to call the assistant principal to thank her for her assistance in this matter, and to confirm that Mrs. Zager called her. As expected, the phone call had been made to the school, and it was just a matter of time before it was finalized in writing.

This whole ordeal surrounding Daniel's progress began to consume my thoughts. "He is really doing well." "He's aware of what's expected of him, and he strives to meet it." "He knows that he can do it!" "He's happy!" "He's also confident!" Wow! "He deserves a chance just like everyone else!" By the time that last thought crossed my mind, there was a big smile on my face. It felt like sunshine was all over me. I was happy for my little boy! It was time for his next level, and change was inevitable!

Over the next few weeks I found myself talking to God about my inner excitement. Sensing that something new was on the horizon, whatever it was, it had to be orchestrated by God, and not by me. He had done a marvelous job thus far, and certainly He still knew what He was doing!

On a day when I was not thinking about it, the long awaited phone call came from Mrs. Zager. Daniel's report card had been corrected to indicate that he was promoted to the third grade. In addition, she was mailing the correction to me to be received by the end of the week. We again discussed his placement, and she still did not have an answer for me. She wasn't familiar with that area of the school, therefore she had no information about the third grade teachers. Although feeling somewhat lost, it was time for me to find a sense of direction for third grade. Unfortunately most of the teachers were still out for the summer. But on the other hand, the office, which also had access to the curriculum could provide me with enough information so that the right decision could be made on Daniel's behalf. In my conversation with one of the administrators, a very key point was made that all third graders would be required to take the statewide assessment test in both reading and math. The test scores would determine whether or not a student passed or failed third grade. Some accommodations would be made for Daniel, but he would still be required to pass the test in order to be promoted to the fourth grade. If a student failed the test they would be required to repeat third grade, and to take the test again. At that moment I questioned the average number of enrollment in the third grade classes. The response was that they were pretty large classes, twenty to twenty-five students, with a teacher, and a teacher's aide. Now considering the size of Mrs. Zager's class, that was going to be a huge difference, and I didn't want him to fall behind. It was time to do some researching for an alternative plan. The idea of standardized testing to determine how much a student learned during the school year was great. But for it to be the determining factor of pass or fail didn't seem fair to me. That might work for him in the future, but not at this moment when he was just coming out of the starting blocks. It was very important that he continued to excel, and to have a fair chance at it!

With that realization, I took into consideration the school that my oldest son was attending. The school used the A Beka curriculum, which is a Bible-based curriculum. It was considered one of the best, and very thorough because it gives a good foundation in phonics, which makes wonderful readers. While thinking about how well my older son did, I was also reminded of my niece who studied the same curriculum from her early elementary school years on into junior high school, and was an honor student. As a matter of fact most children I personally knew who attended an A Beka school did well in school. So I decided to follow my heart and call some of the schools in our area that used this curriculum, including my son's school.

The information discovered was exactly what I needed in order to be educated enough to make a decision. My findings revealed that in addition to a great curriculum, the other unique quality about these schools was that they were private. They were not subject to the public school system. However, they did use standardized testing, but it did not determine whether or not a child passed or failed. These schools were renowned for their students making high test scores, as well as many of them receiving college scholarships. Classes for special needs students included speech and occupational therapists, as well as a modified curriculum. Many of the local businesses financially supported the various intramural sports and extracurricular activities. Most of these schools were also an affiliate of a church or religious organization. There was a registration and book fee, along with a sizeable tuition ranging from four to nine thousand dollars per year. Ouch!

Upon hearing about the tuition, I asked if there were scholarships for students in the special needs classes. It was a pleasant surprise to know that the state's education department provided financial support for special needs students. I was referred to the website to apply. Afterwards, the only step left was to make the decision of a public or private school.

During the next several days we toured one private school after another in hopes to find the best fit for Daniel. At the end of our touring, I was happy with the idea of both of my sons attending the same school. Although they are four years apart, and would not share any classes, it was a good fit for him. So, I called the school and gave them a final okay to add him to their roster. I also called Mrs.

Zager and told her that we would not be returning to Tyndale, and expressed how appreciative we were for how she had impacted our son's life, and gave him a great educational foundation.

I had no idea that Tyndale Elementary would be a part of our lives for only three years. My plan was for the enrollment to continue from kindergarten through sixth grade. We had a great three years there! So much was accomplished! So many lives were impacted! But if I could summarize here the results of putting him in a private school for third grade, let me first start by saying that it was the right choice! Not only did he adjust well, but he also caught on to the new curriculum and its ton of homework. He liked his new teacher, the students, and his new therapists. Speaking of students, there were several new students in this class, therefore he was not the new kid this time. When my daughter learned that the boys would be attending the same school, she asked me if she could attend there also. Since she was not eligible for a scholarship, we would need to pay her tuition out of pocket. Realizing that it was a good idea to put all three into the same private school, I decided that it was a good time for me to return to Corporate America. I applied for a teacher assistant job at the school, and also availed myself to lead praise and worship in the weekly chapel services. The school called me within a few days and told me that a teacher assistant position was available in one of the special education classes. Daniel's class. I accepted the position. My daughter was enrolled into the fifth grade class, and the months that followed were likened to an adventure of a lifetime. The teacher allowed me to implement reading groups for the class. It was my favorite time of the day. The joy of learning was openly expressed by them! And they reminded me that being a special needs student didn't mean that they couldn't excel, but that they just needed a little extra help getting there!

The class consisted of twelve students. Ten of them were boys. They were at such an impressionable age. Although it was no piece of cake, it certainly was not chaotic. Good classroom management makes all the difference in the world! Add the ability to pray over them at the beginning of the day, and there you have the recipe for a successful school year!

Daniel's therapies continued with him seeing the speech and language pathologist twice a week, and the occupational therapist once a week. Their contribution to the student body played a major role in the success of those who received services from them. They were familiar with Daniel's history, and thought that his story was phenomenal. It was always my pleasure to talk to them and to receive feedback about the students. We established friendships. However, later in the school year the occupational therapist resigned.

As the weeks passed, Daniel observed my two older children and their attitude towards doing their homework. It wasn't long before he picked up their study habits. As a matter of fact on most days upon arriving home he'd ask me, "Mom are you going to help me with my homework?" My reply almost always was, "No, daddy will." My husband and I agreed that since I was the teacher assistant for Daniel's class, he would help him with his homework, and I would pitch in only when needed. It worked out well, allowing me to have some separation from him during the day.

An Extraordinary Assignment

This morning I woke up to my favorite day of the week. Friday. It is my favorite day of the week because it ushers me into the weekend, where I can embrace some of life's simplest pleasures. Like staying up past midnight watching movies, or lying in bed under a heavy comforter, listening to rain falling, while enjoying every minute of it, without having to get up for work the next day. Mmmmmm.

The day began as a very normal day. I checked my calendar to make sure that Daniel's next appointment with Dr. Buckley was on it, and afterwards checked the other scheduled events. Although we were at her office each week for Mild Hyperbaric Therapy, she hadn't seen him for an exam in nearly a year, but the day was fastly approaching. I was eager for her to see his progress, as well as to receive our next set of instructions.

Finally upon arriving to work, I took a few minutes to look over some office mail. We were informed that we had a new occupational therapist on board to begin that day. I was also informed that she was looking forward to meeting me because we had quite a bit in common concerning our children.

Shortly after lunch a new, yet very friendly face entered our classroom. She introduced herself as the new occupational therapist. I welcomed her and stated, "We've been anticipating your arrival." I was excited for the students who would benefit from her services. After discussing some of the services that she would provide, the conversation shifted and became even more interesting. She commenced to tell me that, "She had a nine year old daughter with autism, who was a patient of Dr. Julie Buckley. Her daughter began seeing Dr. Buckley in the spring of 2004, and was currently being seen on a monthly basis." She went on to say that, "A mutual friend of ours told her that I had a son who was also being treated by Dr. Buckley for autism, and she'd like to hear my story." I shared Daniel's story with her, not leaving much out: I emphasized the pain of his being misdiagnosed for two years, and finally after receiving a formal diagnosis, having to face a giant that we'd never heard of. I stressed the initial feelings of anger and helplessness. I recalled the pain of having to wake up every morning to this reality instead of remembering it only as a bad nightmare. I talked about his quirky gestures, and the intolerable behavior that nearly got us thrown out of some of our favorite places. At night I cried silently, and turned my pillow over once the tears became to cold to lie in. I also mentioned the headache of sharing the news with family and friends, only to realize that it was too much information for them. She nodded when I spoke of the task of preventing him from embarrassing himself around other children, who would not understand why he was six years old and still wearing a pull-up, as well as the task of finding him a school that would have his best interest at heart, and trusting them enough for me to leave him for six hours. It was even harder realizing that he had never said, " I love you Mommy" or sing 'Happy Birthday to You.' The chaos and ruckus of constant crying and screaming in our once fun-filled, family home. The memory of being exhausted beyond words, and just wanting a good night's rest. The realization that only God could and was able to make Daniel whole again, and that I could not afford to stop believing. And finally, the moment in the checkout line at the neighborhood convenience store that changed it all by just a glimpse at the headline of the morning newspaper.

Our conversation continued as we exchanged stories about Mild Hyperbaric Therapy, supplements, and family outings. Somehow I failed to mention earlier in the conversation that Daniel's first visit with Dr. Buckley was in May 2004. When I finally did mention it, her facial expression changed to that of total amazement. Then she said to me, "Do you realize that both of our children began seeing Dr. Buckley at about the same time? I don't understand what I'm doing wrong. My daughter has had very little improvement, despite the treatment. We've even invested in a Mild Hyperbaric Chamber for our home, so that she can have more frequent sessions, but still we have seen very little improvement. But your son seems to be doing very well with similar treatments. Sheila, what am I doing wrong?"

I then said to her, "Never again say that you're doing something wrong. Living with an autistic child is not easy. I know for a fact that there are parents who love their child, and would have done almost anything to keep them at home, but the needs of the child required them to be institutionalized, or put in a group home. Again these are parents who dearly love their child, but also realize what is best for the child. You are doing what you believe is best for your daughter. I commend you, and you need to commend yourself. You possess a great deal of strength, and you are flexing your muscles every day that you wake up and continue to fight for her."

She then asked me, "Well what did you do that I'm not doing?" I responded, "I got tired of crying. Instead of just crying, I started talking to God about it every day. I needed to tell Him what was happening. I reminded myself that He is my ultimate source of strength, and that He would never tire of listening to me. I also began listening to some of my Pastor's sermons on CD, as well as music that kept me encouraged. Attending weekly services at church became extremely vital to my emotions and sanity. There were times when the praise and worship team would sing, and I knew that the Lord had them "singing over me." I'd often cry through the lyrics as I was reminded of how much He loves me, and that there was nothing too hard for him to do. Releasing the tears allowed me to release all of the stress. It was like fresh rain flowing over me, and afterwards covering me with a blanket of peace. By the time my pastor got up to teach, I was well able to hear him, and receive ultimate strength. I was reminded that God is the creator, which means he created Daniel. So if anyone knew how to get to the heart of the problem and fix it, it was Him.

I remembered a comparison story about automobiles. For example, if I purchased a very expensive luxury automobile, and it malfunctioned, needed maintenance, or repairs, I would not trust it to the hands of my favorite cousin, who likes to work on cars, neither to the neighborhood auto repair shop. I would only take it to the original manufacturer, who knows every fiber of the vehicle, and its original purpose of being created. Well, Daniel certainly is worth more than the finest of automobiles. He's priceless! Therefore inviting God into the matter was the ultimate, right move. He's our creator, the original manufacturer of the human body. And as a result we began to see miracles. I told her I am a born again Christian, meaning that I believe in the Lord Jesus Christ. I believe he died on the cross for the sins of the world that he was buried, and on the third day he rose from the dead with all power in His hand, and now sits in Heaven at the right hand of the Father. I went on to say that he died not only for our sins, but also for our sicknesses and diseases. And today He's still saving and healing those who believe in Him. She looked at me and said, "Sheila I'm Jewish." I responded, "Okay, I understand the Jewish doctrine, but what do you personally need? Because Jesus was more than just a prophet, He was born Savior of the world, and He's already made provision for what you so need---your daughter to be healed." She then shared with me that although she has her personal beliefs about Christianity, she also has friends who are Jews for Jesus, and that she attended their fellowships. I encouraged her to continue, but also extended an invitation for her to be my guest at one of our worship services.

As we wrapped up our conversation, I remembered that Daniel was sitting on the other side of the room laughing and talking with his classmates. So I told her, "By the way, Daniel is in here." "Really? In here?" she excitedly asked. "Yes. There are a total of twelve students in here at the moment, and he's over there among the nine boys. Can you point him out?" She looked fascinated as she tried to point him out! You would have thought we were on a television game show, she was the contestant, I was the host, and Daniel was the new car! After several attempts, I finally said, "Daniel Christie, Please come here." Her eyes were fixed on him as he quickly approached us. "Yes, Mrs. Christie?" He responded. She and I laughed, and then I introduced them. He nearly ran back to his seat to continue his conversation. She wiped her eyes, and said, "I have been so inspired by your story! This is so wonderful. Your son is truly a miracle! There are so many more families who need to hear your story!" As I began to share with her about my role with other families, as an advocate for children with autism, I heard an audible, and unforgettable voice say to me, "It's time to write your book." I immediately responded, "What book?" I then quickly explained to her what I believed I'd just heard. She became very excited and said, "Yes, you have to write a book! People need to know that someone else has gone through this nightmare, and can identify with them. And they especially need to know of your son's recovery!" I then responded, "I said I'd never write a book, because it would require me to relive the shock and pain of this entire ordeal." I told her that in the past, I'd written and recorded songs to raise awareness, and shared Daniel's story while performing live, but it was a summary, not a detail for detail book."

After listening to myself talk, I finally realized that I not only had to write a book, but I needed to continue to reach out to the families who crossed my path each week. Some were referred to me, others were met while out shopping, dining, at school, etc. I'd reached the point where I could recognize an autistic child or adult almost instantly. I would introduce myself and share Daniel's story. If he was with me, it was the icing on the cake. I'd end the conversation by giving them Dr. Buckley's contact information, and exchanging email addresses or phone numbers. It was the best feeling to hear a parent say that, "They didn't know that recovery was possible, yet now, they can help their little one, or loved one." So I told her, "Yes, I'm going to write a book!" We then agreed that we both needed to get back to work. She walked out of the room and returned to her office.

Now although I was very excited about writing a book, there were many questions that I needed answers to such as, what was the name of the book, what was I writing about, and who was my audience? I kept saying out loud, "Lord I will not tell anyone that you told me to do this until I absolutely know that you did." So, for the remainder of the day, I was in expectation of some kind of sign to let me know that I was on the right path.

When we arrived home that afternoon, my children ran from inside the garage into the house in excitement of it being the weekend. They knew that for the next forty-eight hours or so our "weekend only rule" would be active. They could now play video games, watch movies, shoot hours of basketball, and play outside from Friday afternoon through Sunday afternoon. So, my oldest son immediately picked up the basketball and began shooting hoops without even going inside to change his school clothes. My daughter and Daniel ran inside to play video games and I followed them, that is, to the kitchen, to cook dinner. I had a lot on my mind, and I figured that if I cooked dinner first, I could spend the remainder of the evening relaxing and re-visiting the events of the day.

After prepping the food, and finally putting it in the cooking mode, I went outside to hang out with my son while he was playing basketball. When he saw me, he motioned to me to come quickly. He was staring at the sky just above our house. "Mom look! There's a rainbow over our house!" he said. Speaking in a doubtful tone, I responded, "Where do you see a rainbow?" "In the cloud right there. Do you see it?" he asked. "Yes I see it."

As I stood there looking at the cloud, although it was very small, there were very vivid, pretty colors of the rainbow inside of it. I remember having seen a similar cloud back in April 2007, while on the way to a church picnic. The cloud on that particular day formed a shape of a dove, and had the beautiful colors of the rainbow in it. I was so intrigued by it. It was very captivating. By the time I reached for the camera, it had disappeared. So considering having seen a cloud similar to the one that I was staring at, I wasn't too impressed by it. But I couldn't deny that there was a cute little colorful cloud above my house. Nonchalantly, I went back inside to check on dinner.

Moments later I went back outside to be with my son. He immediately stopped playing ball as if he was waiting for me, and said excitedly, "Now look at it!" I detected that he had discerned my lack of interest in the first cloud. However, I cooperatively stood next to him and once again looked up at the sky. This time I could not believe what my eyes were seeing! There was the most beautiful rainbow over my house. It was full, and it seemed close enough for me to touch it. As I stared at it, I realized I could see the end of it. It ended on the fence on the right side of our house. I walked backwards down the driveway while still looking up at the sky, in hopes of seeing where it began. By the time I reached the end of the driveway, I was able to see the beginning of the rainbow. It began on the opposite side of the house, with just a little of it spilling over our privacy fence into the yard next door. I stood speechless and in awe! I'd never in my life seen what my eyes were beholding. As great and vast as a rainbow is, my house was the only one that it was over! In addition, I recalled seeing many rainbows in the sky over our subdivision, but I'm telling you, none of them was ever on my side of the street, let alone only over my house. They were always over the neighbor's house across the street, and they had been for the twelve years that we've lived here.

Eventually I went back inside again to check on dinner. I then began to verbalize what was on my mind. "Lord, why is there a rainbow over my house, and only my house? Is this some sort of sign? If so, what are you trying to tell me? What are you saying to me?" Afterwards within a few seconds it was as if someone rewound a tape recorder and pressed play. Immediately I was reminded of my earlier conversation with God where I was asking Him to "Confirm if He was inspiring me to write this book." When I realized that my prayer was being answered, I asked Him, "Is the title of the book, "A Rainbow over My House" or "There's a Rainbow Over my House?" I didn't feel like either was the title, so I pondered the words in my mind. Within a few minutes I shouted, "Rainbow over My House!" "That's it!" I said. And undoubtedly it agreed with my spirit. I immediately phoned my mother to share with her the events of that day. She was very excited about the news, and then said something

113

very profound. "Sheila, this really is an interesting story." "Why?" I asked. She responded, "It did not rain today, neither last week. In fact it's been more than two weeks, since the last time it rained. So, I wonder where did the rainbow come from?" I felt like answering as Timon would, "I don't wonder, I know." Shortly after ending our phone conversation, my husband arrived home. He saw the rainbow and immediately began taking pictures of it with his cell phone. I brought to his attention the scope of the rainbow. After sharing with him the details of the day, we found ourselves discussing the story of Noah and the Ark, and the purpose of the rainbow, according to the Bible:

God said, "I do set my bow in the cloud, and it shall be for a token of a covenant between me and the earth. And I will remember my covenant, which is between me and you and every living creature of all flesh; and the waters shall no more become a flood to destroy all flesh. And the bow shall be in the cloud; and I will look upon it, that I may remember the everlasting covenant between God and every living creature of all flesh that is upon the earth. (Genesis 9: 13, 15-16) KJV.

We remembered a passage from one of the messages at church that, "The rainbow was for a sign to the people. A covenant or promise that God made to Noah that the earth would never be destroyed again by water." Because God's promises never end, today He still puts the rainbow in the sky to remind us of what He said. Read Noah and the Flood (Genesis 6:5 – 9:17) KJV. In addition, because a rainbow was only over my house, I also believe that it was His way of telling my family and I that we would never see these autism symptoms again. And I believe Him!

Later during dinner, we discussed more of the events of the day, and afterwards I accepted the task of an extraordinary assignment--- To give hope to others by sharing our journey through autism – by writing a book.

It's Your Turn!

Looking back at the past seven years of my life, I realize that having a child with autism was more challenging than I could have imagined. The everyday demand of taking care of Daniel somewhat disguised how tedious and stressful the journey really was. Because most of my time was spent on doctor's visits, therapists, preparing meals, and meeting his every need, I had no time to observe the calendar. My months were not based upon days of the week. Instead, they were based upon his scheduled appointments. It was normal for me to breeze through one month right into the next, because each day was so full of responsibilities. During those times of feeling fatigued, he was my motivation to keep going. However, some days presented a greater battle that well withstood my motivation. It was during these times that I could have thrown in the towel, and said that, "I can't do this anymore. It's just too much! and received an honorable mention and a pat on the back for giving my all. But I'm glad that the story has a different ending. I'll forever be convinced that I did not travel this journey in my own strength. I don't believe that any human being has that kind of strength within himself alone. That kind of strength comes only from the Lord! I'm so glad that He's still providing strength!

I don't believe that I'll ever forget what I experienced on this journey. In fact, there are some things that I don't want to forget. Such as, what I call my list of firsts:

1) *The first time Daniel sang to me, "Happy Birthday to You!"*

2) *The first time his brain and eye muscles worked together allowing him to completely close his eyes to give thanks for our food at dinnertime*

3) *The day he mastered potty training*

4) *The first time he sat in the front passenger seat while I was driving*

5) *His first day of school*

6) *The first time he completely emerged his head under the water in the swimming pool*

7) *His first solo ride on the go-cart*

8) *The first time he dressed himself*

9) *His first visit to Dr. Buckley's office*

10) *His first time playing basketball outside with his older brother, unsupervised*

11) *The first time I took an afternoon nap, and left him up watching a movie and playing with his brother and sister*

12) *The first time that he made his own lunch, and sat and ate it while watching television*

13) *His first visit to the dentist*

14) *The first time he asked the nurse what was she going to do with the needle in her hand*

15) *The first time that he gave the waiter his order at a restaurant*

I could go on because they're more, firsts in Daniel's life. I get so excited just reading this list! It is a huge reminder that recovery from autism is possible, because miracles still happen! And not just for me and my household, but also for you and yours. So are you ready for a miracle? Yes! Super! Great! That's what I want to hear! Because it is your turn now!

You now know my story, and what I experienced on this journey. However, as a dynamite-dose of encouragement, I'd like to give you an update on Daniel. He is now eleven years old, and will enter junior high school in August. He is doing remarkably well. He was mainstreamed into a general education classroom in fourth grade, and defied all of the stereotypes and labels that he'd faced in the past. He is very adamant about studying and making good grades. After school he takes a forty-five minute break, and then does his homework. If he doesn't need my help, he will work independently, later having me to check it. Ninety percent of the time, Daniel tells me that he does not need help with his homework. He is an honor roll student. Keeping up academically with my two older children is what motivates him. He sees the reward of hard work. We continue to see the speech and language therapist for two hours per week, and the occupational therapist for thirty minutes per week. In celebration of his recovery, I have a lengthy "catch up or to do" list of what he's ready to, or need to learn. Although I've made the list, he's already accomplished many of the items on it. For example, he and I along with other relatives climbed Stone Mountain in Atlanta, Georgia last summer. Now, that was not on the list. But he handled it like a pro. He now plays basketball outside with his older brother. For many years Daniel required adult supervision for all outside activities. He's in his second summer of basketball camp, and is becoming a lover of the game. I'm looking forward to his joining the ranks of my two other hoop stars in the house. Learning to roller-skate is on my to do" list, but ever since he fell, he has not been too interested in putting on skates again. I think I'll try a scooter first. Hopefully it will build his interest in learning to skate again.

Daniel is a planner and very meticulous. Before we retire for the evening, he has to know what our plans are for the next day. He prepares his school clothes and backpack in advance. He goes to bed on time without any fuss. No, really! If the family is watching a good movie, he will tell us "good night," and go to bed, with the knowledge that he can finish watching it on tomorrow. He loves structure and order during the week, but loves his video games and movies on the weekend. His favorite place in the whole wide world is the library! I don't know of any human being that loves the library as much as Daniel! I made a library in our home, but I couldn't keep up with his desire to read. Although I continue to buy books, he still requests to go to the library. When at the library, he literally sits or kneels on the floor for hours reading book after book. One can easily tell that he is "at home."

What I've told you so far about Daniel describes a very serious and focused child. And that he is. But there is also a humorous side of him that livens up the house. He loves to laugh. His laugh is so contagious until it will make you laugh, even if you're in another part of the house! Just hearing him laugh makes you laugh. Many days I've stopped what I was doing just to go and see what movie or television show he was watching. Two of his favorite shows are "Wipeout" and "America's Funniest Videos (AFV)." They fall in line second to "Dinosaur King." Daniel at times, can also be a prankster. You can count on him to tickle your ear if you fall asleep on the sofa, while watching television. The first time he did this to me, I slapped my ear several times before I realized that nothing was crawling on me. You should have seen him laughing. My response was, "Hey! Who taught you how to do that?" He looked at me and boldly said, "Me!" He will also try to tickle your feet with his, if you're not paying attention. He loves to play our home version of Family Feud. At school he enjoys playing dodge ball, tag, and kickball. He is a great conversationalist, asking many questions, and not afraid to share his personal opinion.

One afternoon my oldest son and daughter came to me, as if they had a private meeting among themselves and asked, "When is

Daniel going to start doing chores?" Honestly, I had not thought about it, but recognized that it was a great idea! And so, he received his first assignment of emptying the waste baskets in the bathrooms every other day. Vacuuming the floor was soon added to his list of responsibilities. He took pride in doing his chores well, and made sure that we praised him for it.

Oftentimes if I needed to run an errand, I would ask Daniel to ride with me. He was good company. I could also guarantee that there'll be some good riding music. He sets in the repeat mode singer, Maurette Brown Clarks' song, "Has God Done Anything for You." He also enjoys the music of recording artists, Canton Jones, Toby Mac, Israel Houghton, BeBe and CeCe Winans, Fred Hammond, and Tye Tribbett. During our Sunday morning drive to church he enjoys listening to the Don Moen and Friends radio show. He has such an ear for music that when I purchase a new CD, his response to it lets me know whether or not I wasted my money. He is leading a wonderful life! I'm just sitting back enjoying the view. It's more breathtaking than the sun setting over the ocean in the Caribbean on a beautiful summer evening. Ummm.

What a wonderful feeling! It belongs to you too! Just envision yourself there! I can see you there! There, as in freedom! Recovery from every sign and symptom of autism! Your loved one whole and well! Your family experiencing the life that you dream of! Yes! Not only is it possible, but as the kids say, "Tag, you're it!" I declare that, "It's your turn!" "Go for it!"

Finest Resources

When our autism journey began, support groups were very scarce. Now they're nearly everywhere, including schools, churches, corporate offices, and even sporting events. Information that was once unavailable regarding the onset and treatment of autism is now in books and manuals, both in bookstores and online. Autism conferences are held all over the United States and abroad, throughout the year.

Because I'm not a doctor, I cannot make any recommendations; however, there are lots of great resources available. I'd like to mention just a few:

1) **AutismResearchInstitute.com (Defeat Autism Now!)**

English: 1-866-366-3361

Espanol: 877-644-1184 ext 5

2) **Healing Our Autistic Children by Dr. Julie A Buckley**

(Purchase at Barnes and Noble or Amazon.com)

3) HealAutismNow.Org (HEAL! Foundation)

Co-founded by Dr. Julie Buckley and Robert and Leslie Weed

4) RainbowOverMyHouse.com (The Book)

(Online Support and Advocacy; I'd like to hear about your progress!)

5) Special Diets for Special Kids (GF/CF Cookbook)

Forget Me Not

I took the time to acknowledge some of those who were very instrumental as a source of inspiration and encouragement in the writing of this book. Others were a pillar of strength throughout the actual healing process. They were and forever will be close to my heart. But there is one sole person who literally sustained me! Breathed life into me! Carried me, everyday! Kept my emotions in tact so that I would not go crazy! He lifted up my head when I wanted to hold it down. He stilled my spirit when all around me seemed tumultuous. He gave me a future and a hope. I reference Him throughout the book, but I want to end with elaborating more about Him and His awesomeness! I'm referring to the Lord Jesus Christ, my source of hope and faith. Daniel's healer! The healer!

Now before you think I'm religious, let me speak up and say that, "I am not religious." I don't believe I can only talk to God on Sundays, neither do I believe I can only hear about Him at church. I'm not persuaded I have to wait until a certain time to get his attention; neither do I believe I have to work for his love.

As a little girl, my Sunday school class sang a song about Jesus' love for me. And they would end it by saying that, "The Bible tells me so."

It's true, the Bible does tell us so, in John 3:16: "For God so loved the world that he gave his only begotten son, that whosoever believeth in him should not perish but have everlasting life." The bottom line is that God loves you, your family, and your loved one who has autism, and any other sickness or disease. And he want you to know he has made a way for you to be healed by his son dying on the cross for our sins and the penalties of sin: sickness, disease, poverty, etc. We do not have to work for his love, nor healing. We only must believe that he is God, and that he is our healer. He is a very loving and merciful God. He loves us, his creation. And he has provided for us to live a good life! Howbeit, we can only live that good life by allowing him to show us how to do it. He must be the one in charge because he knows what's best for us, and what will really bring us the joy we so desire. There is a place in our heart that only he can fill, and if we substitute it with anything else, we will live our lives in search of fulfillment. We will always feel like something is missing, which is why neither money, nor male and female relationships, nor cars and houses can fill that void. They are only mere substitutes that provide temporary happiness, but the joy that Jesus brings is everlasting! He wants to be your Lord and Savior, and to have the opportunity to prove his love to you. When you receive Jesus as Lord and Savior, you also receive his promise of healing. Remember, He died for our sins and sicknesses.

If you don't know Jesus as your Lord and Savior, I would like to take this opportunity to introduce you to him. As you simply pray this prayer he will come into your heart and give you a brand-new life: "Lord Jesus, I believe that you are the Son of God. I believe that you died on the cross for my sins. I believe that you arose, and are alive today. I ask that you will forgive me of all of my sins, cleanse my heart, and make me a new person in you right now. I receive you as my Savior and Lord. Thank you for loving me. In your name I pray. Amen."

If you believed this and just prayed this prayer, congratulations! You are now a "new creature" in Christ. Your brand new life in him just began! If you are currently a member of a church where the Bible is taught, and Jesus is exalted as Lord, it is important that you let someone know of your decision. If you are not a member of a Bible teaching church, it is important that you find a church to attend in your community, where you can continue to learn about Jesus and this wonderful life that you have begun. I would also love to hear from you at RainbowOverMyHouse.com.

The days ahead of you are far greater than your past! It is an exciting time for you and your family, and I celebrate with you! Each day take time to thank God not only for the progress you see, but also for what you are yet believing Him to do. Healing is often a process, but while you are waiting, have great expectation! You must believe, by faith, what you didn't believe before, or thought impossible, and become excited at the realization that something so great and wonderful is happening to you and your family! There is nothing impossible with God, for with God all things are possible to him that believeth! You have every reason to hope, because it is possible! Have faith in God!

Notes

Chapter 2 http://www.healautismnow.org

Chapter 12 Autism Facts http://www.healautismnow.org

About the Author

Sheila Clayton Christie works with special needs elementary age children at Cedar Creek Christian School. Her love for children and the desire to see them and their families lead productive lives lead her to become an advocate for children with autism. The support that she provides has been the reason that many families have found the strength to believe and work towards recovery for their own loved one. Sheila is also a worship leader, recording artist and songwriter, and a conference speaker. She resides in North Florida with her family, Richard, Courtney, and Daniel.

Made in the USA
Lexington, KY
26 January 2013